OSIER CULTURE

AND

BASKET-MAKING

A study of the basket-making craft in South West County Antrim

Patrick Smyth

First published in 1991 by
Patrick Smyth, Marymount, Lurgan, Co. Armagh

© Patrick Smyth

Cover picture by Patrick Smyth

All rights reserved. No part of this publication may be reproduced, stored in a retrieval system or transmitted in any form or by any means electronic, mechanical, photo copying, recording, or otherwise without the prior permission of the copyright owner, given in writing.

Printed by The Universities Press (Belfast) Limited

Booksellers' enquiries:
P. Smyth, Telephone Lurgan (0762) 323098

This publication has been assisted by a grant from the Ulster Local History Trust.

A number of photographs from the Green collection of the Ulster Folk & Transport Museum have been included by permission of the Trustees of the Museum. The pictures were taken sometime between 1918 and 1930 and it has been found most difficult to identify those who posed for them. It is known that in the past strangers to the district found the basketmaking people around Aghagallon and Ballinderry generally camera-shy and very reticent. Stand-ins may have volunteered for the photographer. The first picture from the collection which has been reproduced features two men, each with a potato basket, and one in the middle with a yeast hamper. (I have said 'with' and not 'making', since they are obviously posing.) The broad white ribs in the potato baskets, which are fir timber, indicate that the photograph is a fairly early one; fir ribs were dispensed with later on. From left, the men might be one of the Mulhollands of Gawley's Gate, Joe Russell or Paddy Hannon, and Jack Mallon. Everyone agrees about Jack but there is no unanimity about the others.

Photograph from the Ulster Folk Museum Green Collection.

Preface

A few years ago when the author published *Memories of Old Lurgan*, we in this museum found especially interesting his article on basket-making on the shores of Lough Neagh. We encouraged him to find out more about the industry. Because he is a local man and knows many of the people who were involved in it, he has been able to piece together many details about the firm and its workers. Too often accounts of such craft industries have been concerned with tools and techniques rather than organisation, marketing and working conditions. The initial draft of this publication provoked further questions from Megan MacManus, the curator responsible for the study of crafts and occupations at this Museum. In searching for answers to them, Pat Smyth has produced a portrait of a firm that flourished in a country district between the two World Wars. He has placed it firmly in its social and economic context. We are indebted to him for this valuable study and hope that it will make more people in Northern Ireland aware of the vanished life of their communities.

W.H. Crawford
Keeper of Material Culture
Ulster Folk & Transport Museum

Introduction

Early this century, a working man set up a small factory for the manufacture of baskets at Aghagallon, which is in the south-west corner of County Antrim near Lough Neagh's banks. In it he provided constant employment for about 30 men until the outbreak of the Second World War in 1939. The founder, James Mulholland, had previously made a precarious living by fishing on Lough Neagh in season and making baskets at home for his parents who hawked potato baskets around local market towns and sold yeast skeps to a Belfast merchant. This had been a long established family custom.

A detailed study of the Mulholland enterprise forms the basis of this book but in order to evaluate it the socio-economic history of the locale has had to be examined. It was known that osier culture and the related craft of making baskets and other items of wickerware had been carried on in the area already mentioned for a very long time indeed, but not very much else was known. With the enthusiastic backing of various elder residents a comprehensive and detailed account of every aspect of the cultivation of willow rods, the harvesting and preparation of the material, and the intricate work of making basketware has now been compiled. It has been a fascinating study and it casts new light on many facets of rural life around Aghagallon in the early twentieth century.

Before embarking on a recital of the technical but absorbing details of the Mulholland enterprise an attempt has been made to set the scene for James Mulholland's entry by outlining the historical and geographical features of the area in general terms. There follows a rehearsal of personal stories, recited by four local octogenarians, which are of particular value because they combine to provide a chilling picture of the abject poverty and the misery which prevailed locally when the basket factory was founded. The phrase 'poverty trap' was not in common usage in south-west Antrim in the days preceding the First World War, possibly because as one elder has put it, "Everybody was in the same boat. There was no money anywhere". In other words, the whole way of life of a whole rural community was a life of poverty and there was just no way out of it. To complete the picture an account of what went on contemporaneously a few miles away in Glenavy parish has been included. Comparisons have been made and the findings should be of interest. Finally, the Bavarian scene has been examined. Bamberg, which the Germans term 'the dream city', has been visited and described. The area is the heartland of the German horticultural and basket-making industries – industries which are still thriving whereas osier culture and basket-making on the banks of Lough Neagh seem close to extinction.

The History and Geography of the Area

In post-Plantation times the Seymour Conways, Marquesses of Hertford, were landlords of 60,000 acres of land in south Antrim, one of the biggest estates in Ireland stretching from the Crumlin river to the Lagan and from Derriaghy to Lough Neagh. Gawley's Gate where James Mulholland was born was once the gateway to the Earl of Hertford's extensive deerpark but it is now only a small road junction with a pub and a sub-post-office.

South-west Antrim was once the land of the great oakwood and the number of adjoining townlands therein all prefixed 'Derry' ('Oakwood') are a relic of those bygone days. The rich timberlands were the prizes given to the Undertakers who were appointed by the Crown in Plantation days to drive out the Irish and replace them with English settlers. Some of the natives were allowed to settle in the boglands. Undertakers were not permitted to let them settle on 'hard bottom' land.

People of English origin had most of the big farms locally in James Mulholland's day, but most of the smaller holdings were in the hands of people of Irish extraction who were paying land purchase annuities to English landlords. Cottier houses erected on farms were let to working-class people. A lucky few had tenancies of labourer's cottages. These were the only dwellings which were referred to as 'cottages' in local parlance, hence it would not be quite appropriate to refer to 'a cottage industry'.

It would be difficult to visualise a more depressed area than Lough Neagh's banks in the early part of the 20th century. Those who claimed ownership of the fishing rights on Lough Neagh were constantly harrying the fishermen who, it must be said, refused to pay attention to any regulations. The few sizeable farmers within walking distance of Gawley's Gate mostly had family labour. Some labourers attended hiring fairs and migrated from the Montiaghs but the terms offered by hirers were singularly unattractive, say, £18 a half year with board, circa 1920.

Boat-hauling on the now disused Lagan canal provided an outlet for some men who had been able to raise the price of a horse (50 shillings, i.e. £2.50). More than one generation of some families were boathaulers. Other men got work 'on the bank' as barge men, lock-keepers and labourers on canal maintenance. Jim, Pat, John, Ned and Joe Lavery of Derryhirk (all brothers) John and Paddy McVeigh (brothers) of Aghalee, John's sons, Bob and Jack; Pat's sons, Danny and Joey; John and Pat Creaney (brothers) of Derryclone; Cyril Healey of Cranagh; several members of the O'Neill family of Derryhirk; Jamie, Vincent, Eugene, Frank, Gerald, Jimmy and John Douglas

3

of 'Blow Cottage', Aghagallon; (James was the father; the others were his sons); George Fegan and his sons, George and Eddie of Turtle Dove Lock; Dan Agnew and his sons; Eugene Heaney of Cranagh, Felix McStravick and Harry O'Rawe are other names which I have been given. The list is probably not complete.

The cottage (*sic*) industry of handloom weaving of flax had died out shortly before Mulholland started up his factory, but many local women were doing 'white work' (thread-drawing and hemstitching) as outworkers for Lurgan or Magheralin linen handkerchief factories. A few Aghagallon women wrought in these factories, but there was no public transport, and only those who could afford a bicycle could get there. As well, competition from workers who lived within range of the mill horn in tied houses owned by the linen lords, and who constituted an ample pool of labour, left rural dwellers out in the cold. Many Lurgan textile factories had such a big pool of reserve labour that, from the unemployment benefit scheme commenced in 1912, they always kept a group temporarily stopped. They arranged for all their workers to take it in turn to go 'on the buroo'. When those who were signing-on had drawn out their benefit they were reinstated in the factory, and others were 'put on the buroo' – pawns on their master's chessboard. As outworkers, women got only a penny or two per dozen for handkerchiefs which they processed, and very often they had to sit up at night to meet their employer's schedule.

The extensive area of peat bogs extending along the lough shore, known as the Montiaghs, were the principal source of fuel for local residents. Most farmers had turbary rights, i.e. the ownership of a small area of bog and the right to cut turf. The intricacies of making mud turf are described later in this book. Mud turf is altogether different from spade turf.

Around the lough shore, turf men, fish men, hen men, rag men, and other itinerant dealers proliferated and moved around on foot or in 'springcarts' between the wars. All the occupiers of the wee whitewashed thatched cabins which dotted the shores of Bartin's Bay from Derryclone Point to Gawley's Gate had a miserable existence in the early twentieth century. The little cabins enhanced the scenery, and would have been an artist's delight, but they were whitewashed walls of misery for the inhabitants. With earthen floors, tiny windows, primitive furniture, chaff palliasses for bedding, and without running water, indoor toilets, gas or electricity, hardship prevailed. "There was money for nothing and nobody had anything," is how one octogenarian summed it all up.

The story of Mulholland's factory is, of course, only a brief episode in the long history of the basket-making craft in the area. No one seems to know how old the craft really is. Possibly it is as old as civilisation. Indeed, according to the German basket museum authorities, basket-making is of pre-historic origin. It is therefore, not surprising to find that it featured in the earliest census and ordnance

This picture is published courtesy of the Ulster Folk Museum Green Collection. John Joe McCartan, Selshion, circa 1930, is featured harvesting rods. They say that John Joe grew the finest osiers in the land, the double-eyed Irish rod.

survey records relating to Aghagallon and Ballinderry in south-west Antrim. As long ago as 1802, one writer mentioned a celebrated maker of baskets who was found at Kilwarlin, Moira, (about four miles from Aghagallon) "who made a wide range of basketware from strong clothes baskets to elegant services for deserts and fruit baskets equal to anything imported from France".

Ordnance maps of the 1830s featured osier beds at George's Island, Moss Vale, Bog Head, Derrynaseer and Poobles also around Lough Beg and Lower Ballinderry, County Antrim.

Census notes relating to Ballinderry mention William, Jane, and Margaret Dornan of Ballinderry and John and James Magee, Lurgill, as basket-makers; Arthur Lavery and Henry Lochert of the same address are down as hamper makers; James Garland, Lurgill as basket-maker; James and Ellen Brankin, Montiaghs, Aghagallon, as white basket-makers; William McKeveney, same address, as basket-maker.

Other women included in the census of the locality are down as 'needlework'. These places are shown on the centre page map which has been included in this book.

The mention of white baskets is of particular significance. This shows that there has always been two strands: baskets made of green or unpeeled osiers and the peeled rod variety. Traditionally Aghagallon basket-makers mostly used locally grown unpeeled osiers and made strong baskets, but some families specialised in fancy baskets made from peeled home grown osiers or imported white rods. The writer recalls two sets of brothers with identical names, James and Willie Mulholland, one pair made potato baskets and yeast hampers only, using unpeeled locally grown osiers, the other pair made fancy baskets from fine white rods. The parties lived only half a mile apart. A stranger lacking local knowledge would find that confusing. It is indeed a tangled skein. Contemporaneously Willie and James Mulholland of 'the Gate', i.e. Gawley's Gate made potato baskets and yeast skeps. Willie and James Mulholland of the Cottages, Derrymore, no relations, specialised in fancy baskets made of fine white rods, as did another family at Ballinderry, called Crossey.

To up-date our knowledge of the socio-economic history of the Aghagallon area four articulate local people have rehearsed their experiences of the period from 1915 onwards. Their parents were people who had neither money nor assets and the height of their ambition was to get a living. A bare living was the best that they could hope for and opportunities for further education or employment were non-existent. All four are in the sear and yellow leaf.

The Hired Boy

Here Alfred Grant describes the life of drudgery which he abandoned in despair before he got a job in Mulholland's 'workshop' (as he calls it).

"I was just 14, and I had only left school. I hadn't any work, or a penny in my pocket. Times were hard in them days. My mother was having bother keeping me. This man asked me, one day, would I give him a day's work. I said I would, for I badly needed money.

"I asked him what I would have to do, and he told me he would show me when I went. 'I'll tell you in the morning' was what he said. He had a wee bit of ground in the moss (Montiaghs) and when I went in the morning he said he had corn to harrow. He asked me to take one end of a wee harrow to help him to carry it. It was a wee light seed harrow, with short pins. A wee three-bhul harrow.

"I helped him down to the field with it. He had a rein-cord as well, and when we got to the corn-field he tied one end of the rope to the harrow, and gave me the other, which he told me to put over my shoulder. He showed me how to pull it, and where to go. On and off he gave me a hand. We were at it all day. There was about an acre in the plot and we harrowed it all. I was tough at that time. I had had plenty of experience of hard work when I was at school – helping my father to make mud turf and draw them home, and milking, and driving the horse in the cart, and putting the harness on and off him, and things like that. At the end of the day and it was a long one – he gave me one and six, that would be $7^1/2$p.

"When we had nearly finished, my father arrived with another man, a dairy farmer from the Tansy. He had heard I was strong and a good milker, and he had come to hire me. He offered £18 and my keep for six months' work. My father asked me would I go and I said I would. The man said he needed a good milker, and I was glad to hear it, for I was a dandy milker. I could have held my own with anyone – and maybe I still could.

"I went to him on a Sunday night, that was 11th May 1919. I started next morning – the 12th May. It was about 12 miles from home. I had an old bicycle that cost me thirty shillings, and I was paying sixpence a week off. When I got to the farm at the Tansy, the man was looking out for me. He called his wife out and said, 'I want you to meet our new boy.' His wife was a very kindly woman. She shook hands with me and welcomed me. Then she said. 'I'll be good to you and I hope you will be good to us.' She made me tea, and gave me as much bread as I could eat. When I had finished, the man reached up above his head in the kitchen and pulled down a ladder, which he then set up. Then he climbed up into the loft, and told me to follow him.

"It was a lovely snug wee loft, with a nice single bed

and things. There was a candlestick and a new candle, and a box of matches. He asked me did I smoke, and when I said I didn't he said, 'That's a good job. If you are lighting the candle be very careful, for you are close to the thatch and you could put the whole place up in flames.' I was *very* careful.

"He said, 'Your bedtime is half-nine and you will rise at half-five. I'll call you and I wouldn't want to have to call you twice.' He had 18 cows, and I had to have the milk at Ballinderry station for the twenty past eight train every morning. I took it in a keg, with the horse and cart. It would have been nearly two miles to the station.

"Before I went to bed the first night I had a walk around. When I got to the back of the haggard, out of sight, I climbed up a big ash tree to see if I could see home. I went right up to the topmost branch and I was swaying like a bird, but all I could see was Rams' Island and the lough – no home. I cried then, for I had never been away before and I was very lonely.

"One day we had to dip the sheep. The man handed me an old shirt before we started and said, 'Give me your shirt and put that one on instead. We have to watch the tics.' I did as I was told and when we had finished I had a good wash before I put my own shirt on again. That night was the only time I lit the candle. I wakened up in the middle of the night with a terrible pain in my oxter. When I lit the candle I couldn't see what it was but I 'hoked' with my thumb nail, and brought out bits of an insect. I couldn't get it all out, but I stopped the bad pain. Next morning, the man and his wife looked under my arm and they said it was a tic. The woman dosed it with iodine, and I never looked behind me. Wasn't I lucky I didn't get poisoning?

Brankinstown man, Alfred Grant, skilled turf cutter, retired postman and retired basketmaker, produces a potato basket which he has just made from locally grown osiers in 1989, some 70 years after he made his first one. Alfred's prodigious memory is illustrated in the pages of this book. Photo: P. Smyth.

"I stayed the six months, but I was homesick the whole time. I used to get home for an hour of a Sunday. We usually quit work about half-six in the evening, and I had nowhere to go, and I knew nobody. I never brought anybody in. I don't think them people would have liked me to have brought anybody about the house. I got the best of food – beef every day nearly – but I never was able to eat much, I was that homesick. I just knocked about the fields and haggard in the evenings, glad to give a hand with anything to pass the time.

"When I left, I never went back. Some people wondered at that for they had been very good to me. Even when I got older and had a motor-bike I never went. I just couldn't go back. I had been that homesick all the time.

"After that I got a job with a farmer at George's Island, but him and me had a dispute over pay. He was giving me 15 shillings a week and he went to reduce it to twelve. I left.

"My mother was very upset. 'What *are* you going to do?' she said. 'Where *will* you get another job?'

"I said, 'I don't care. I'm not going to work for that money' nor I didn't.

"I got a job at Mulholland's a wee while after that, and I stayed nearly 20 years."

A traditional potato basket in an indoor setting. Photo P. Smyth

Making Mud Turf at Loughmoney

Harvesting turf for fuel from the local peat bogs has always been an important feature of life in the area where Mulholland's basket factory was set up. Here is Alfred Grant's riveting account of the hardships which had to be endured when he and his father made turf on a contract basis in season when he was young. The story provides a useful insight into the background to Alfred's basket-making career.

"From I was a wee fellow I followed my father when he was cutting turf in the moss and after school I would have learned wee bits and pieces about it. Our plot of moss was down the Feather Bed, at Loughmoney some people call it. There was supposed to be no bottom in Loughmoney. If you went down in it you would go on down to New Zealand or Australia!

"I started to cut turf on my own when I married. I think it would have been about 1932. I had to get a winter's firing for myself and having been used to watching my father when I was a young fellow, and seeing what he had done, I followed his footsteps. He always picked out a nice spot in the bog where he would start and cut. So I burned a nice wee bit first. That was to make the turf easier cut with the spade. Burning was against the law. I was even caught by the police myself one time and it cost me £3-10-0. Times wasn't too good, mind you, that time. I was in an awful transaction at the time, how I would get the fine paid. So eventually I got it gathered up and I kept it in the house and there was a policeman here and he was called Wilton and he came down here for the fine. And he said, 'I have called for the fine, but I hope you haven't got it for me.' And I says 'Why?' and he says 'Because I would like to take you in.' So my wife heard (she was living at the time) and she says 'What's that you say Mr. Wilton?'

"He said, 'I hope he hasn't the fine for me, for I would love to take him with me' and she said 'God forbid that that would happen.' Anyway I paid the fine and we had a bit of a laugh, you know.

"I remember another fellow who wrought beside me and he was always watching for the police because he saw what had happened to me and he always took an old tin can with him with a bit of live turf in it and he used this to light his pipe and one day when he was going home for his dinner he laid that can down on its side in the moss with the mouth towards the wind. And with the wind blowing into the mouth of the can, that lit the moss as he wanted it to do and he had it burning, then if the police had a come he wasn't there and he would have made it out to be an accident.

"This meant that when he came back from dinner the burning was done. One day when he got back and the moss was burning he saw Mr. Wilton watching and he ran as fast as he could and he got his shovel and he started beating out the fire and throwing water on it from the drain. He had knocked the can into the drain before Wilton got over and demanded what he was doing and he said, 'Well, you might ask. This was all right when I went for my dinner and look at it now – and even some of my turf has been burned.' He had the presence of mind to bluff Wilton that somebody else had lit the moss on him and Wilton just threw off his tunic and fell to and helped him to put it out and said nothing.

"After you burn off the grass you start and cut with a good sharp spade (not a special one: just a good one) and you set the sods out on your bank and in about a week's time you stand them up in twos and there's a set on them, the way they're cut, that they lean against one another the way a stook of corn would do. In a week's time then again you would turn them into sevens. Put four in the bottom and three on the top and you let them be, maybe, for a week or ten days. In good drying weather they soon dry, so after that you put them in 'winrows' (what you call a winrow) and that winrow is about a yard long and the old style of putting them in, the Moss man's style, is that you put the end of that winrow towards Lurgan. And you'll maybe, ask why. Why they always put the end towards Lurgan? Well, there's always more rain comes out of Lurgan than any other part. Do you see? And when you have that end towards Lurgan it doesn't hit the broadside of the winrow – therefore, you put it so the turf gets less wet. It's maybe, laughable to other people but it's true. We have proved it.

"So after you have that done – it used to be that you put them in clamps. That was a square clamp. You put them flat on the ground and you built them up till about five foot in the air (in height) So, we changed all that. Time came that people learned a wee bit more and now we put them in 'rickles' they call it – they are pillars. And you stand them on their end on the ground first, and they're round and you build them a wee bit open – the way you would break the joint in brickwork and there the wind blows through and the sun gets at them and they dry better.

"The sod is what they call the top cutting off the moss. It's cut with the spade and whenever you have that top cutting done you could take another cutting or two off that. What they call cut turf, but you need a spade with a lug on one side of it for to cut the turf right, but it is not often done in this bog for it's not every sort of bog that suits that cut turf. That means that we have to get into the drain and put wet mud out.

"The making of the mud turf is like this. When you go to the bank (the turf bank) you take off your trousers and you have an old pair with you cut off below the knees that you put on, and you are in your bare feet. And many's the time it was cold enough at half past seven in the morning, and maybe a wee white frost in the latter end of May. And you went in there, after you had stripped and put on 'the old mud britches'. Many a time I think of it when the footballers came out on a bad day; but, of course, they can run about. The mud was a colder job than the footballer has, for he can run, but we had to stay in the water. And you turned over that first 'spitten' in the drain with a spade. And it was broken up with a graip that had three prongs on it. There was a track put down the middle of it, and it was turned over with the spade, and it was graiped fine, just like wet cement. Just the same as cement. And you daren't throw it – you daren't throw it just out anywhere. There was a way you had to leave it along the brow of the drain, along the bank you called it.

"And every bit that you laid out you had to slide it back because if you hadn't 'a-slid' that back in liquid form it would never have lifted in turf. But when you slid that back it lifted clean off that grassy bed. And you didn't burn any bank that you were going to put mud out on. You left the grass on it and slid the mud back on it, so that it would lift clean off it later.

"That link or square that you were working, that was five yards or six wide and it had to be the same measurement at the back. When you put that mud back in liquid form and it just was the same as cement coming out of a lorry and you had that square and you levelled it with the back of your shovel and when you had it real level, about four or five inches deep, you baked (shaped) that with your hands. We will say 18 inches long, the turf, and about $3^{1}/_{2}$ or four inches wide. The joint was about five yards in length. You would have baked 19 turf in width across that. And if you got well down the drain you would have been 32 foot back when you had a plot of mud done.

"A moss man who knew what he was talking about had no call to count. He could have told anybody how many turf was in the plot without counting them. If you had a five yard joint and three men in it, usually they would have put out three joints a day. That was some work.

"You baked it in the shape or form of turf in the liquid and it was nice to look at, when done right. You had to walk back all the time as you baked with your hands. You were pulling (working) from' the drain outwards and when you finished baking you were out on the dry ground and generally when you were baking the last row you went down on your knee. I would always have made a nicer row, to finish, by going down on my knee. Some people used to laugh at me, but I like to finish off neat.

"When you had finished baking you trimmed the back end of your plot of mud with your shovel and when you had that done neighbours would have been out of a Sunday to see how other people were getting on. You had to be a tradesman. It was a trade of its own.

"We started at half past seven and the people you were working for would have brought tea at ten o'clock. That was one thing. You got plenty of food. You got tea and bread at ten o'clock and then the dinner came about half-twelve and more tea at four. Three times you got tea and bread. Sometimes it wasn't tea, but you were better with tea. A dinner of potatoes didn't do well if you were in the mud. If you were down in the water potatoes weren't good for you.

"And I'll tell you another thing that was very dangerous: cabbage. If anybody had brought you cabbage, even the doctors didn't allow you to eat cabbage. I can remember well there was a man called James Lavery. They brought him cabbage and buttermilk for his dinner and he ate it and that night he took severe cramps and he was at death's door – he was nearly away with it. They thought he was going to die. And a warning went out around the district never to drink fresh buttermilk or eat green cabbage. I myself drank fresh buttermilk and at eleven that night when I came home out of the mud, I took cramps too but I wasn't as bad as James Lavery.

"If the plot of mud (turf) that had been baked had a' got a dry night, or maybe the next day dry as well, they would have got what we called 'a kind of a dry skin' on them, and your turf never looked behind them after that, and in a week's time you lifted them. And the marks on the mud that you had made with your hands, you nicked them with the spade. Then you lifted them with your bare hands, and you set them on their ends. And another thing too – you set them on the ground singly in rows. You wrought with your hands, but you should have had your back 'toast' (towards) Lurgan, for to get the back of your turf facing the right way; again, so as for them not to get the heavy rain. That was what you called 'lifting' and when you done that, in a week or so's time you turned round and you turned them upside down, two in the bottom and one on the top (no name for that) and the next thing you done was four in the bottom and three on the top. That was the next shift – 'sevens'.

"After that, you were back on the sod system again; you put them in winrows. The way you would have done with sods. Then into the clamps. Then into pillars (rickles). And the next shift was the drawing home. But you never drew the rickles home till 'Murtie's month'. I'm a brave wee age now and I never could understand that. The old people called it 'Murtie's month', October, for drawing home the turf. I never heard who Murtie was – I don't know where the old people got 'Murtie's month' but that was the time to draw them home.

"My father drew them home with a donkey and cart. He had no house for them and they had to be stacked outside (out of doors). He built a stack in the haggard where the hay was stacked. I built a stack many's the time myself and, I'll tell you better than that. I remember the Lappins of the Moss, there were three or four brothers of them, great turf men, great mud men. They all went to America eventually, but before they went they put turf out and sold it. They put them on the Feather Bed (road) in stacks and the stacks were six yards by two wide and they brought out Robert Graham, the auctioneer, and he auctioned them stacks at the Feather Bed. People came from as far away as Crewe Hill and from above Aghalee some of them too, and they bought them at 30 shillings a stack. And they drew (carted) them away with big horses and big carts the sort the moss men had never seen – big deep carts – no turf racks on them. Some turf men did have racks. You never put racks on a donkey cart. It wouldn't have been able to pull a full load out of the moss because of the soft ground. It was near hand where they had to draw them to, and working out of the moss you didn't need too heavy a load.

"I scarcely ever missed cutting the winter firing in the moss in my life. I was always with my father when he did it and since I was married I have never missed. I cut them this year (1990) as usual. That would be near sixty years Without a break since I first cut winter firing for the wife and myself. There's nothing to beat a turf fire."

Author's Note: Some other seasoned makers of mud turf maintain that neither potatoes nor cabbage ever fizzed on them. Obviously constitutions differ.

Stack of osiers grown in 1990 by the Mulholland family (at Derrynaseer Aghagallon)

Dodging the Bailiffs at Bartin's Bay

Retired fisherman John McAlinden, now in his eighties, resides in a modern bungalow on the edge of Bartin's Bay from whence he has an uninterrupted view of Tolan's Point and the Tyrone shore around the Battery. He knows every mood of the lough and wryly recalls the days of his youth when 'nobody had a penny for there was no money for anything'. Here he gives us a vivid insight into the manner in which the Lough Neagh fishermen had to use their wits to survive.

"My father was a fisherman and his father before him. I was on a fishing boat from I was nine years old, that would have been in 1917. Mostly after school, but sometimes I didn't bother going to school at all. My grandfather shipped his own fish. He took them to the railway station, with a pony and van. They all went to Billingsgate market. Latterly, James Edward was the main man. He set up a kind of a depot and collected in the eels from all of us and took them to the railway. He bought at so much and got what he could for them. He became the important one then.

"In my day, they made about fifteen or sixteen shillings a stone. There was talk of some getting £1; some of the Tyrone men claimed they got £1, but we never got that much on this side of the Lough. It was trout in the springtime and then it wore on to the setting of the lines for eels later on in the summertime. At first all I did was keep the live bait alive. They were kept in a tank in the boat and they needed fresh water to keep them living. At one time it came in that it all had to be live bait. It hadn't always been like that. I don't know who started that carry-on, or how it started. The fish just wouldn't take dead bait. Small live perch were used. You had to watch how you put the hook in them so as not to kill them. They had to stay alive on the hook so you put it in near the tail.

"We used eel lines. A line would have had maybe 300 hooks. Some of them had 400. It was a tricky job hitching the hooks on the lines and then layering the lines in the boxes, so that they didn't get snarled up when they were being laid. They were always laid in the evening and lifted early in the morning. We never had anything but an open boat, no cabin, no engine – nothing but the oars. If the weather was too bad you just didn't go out. For a long time we had no oilskins or anything like that, and Wellington boots hadn't been heard tell of – no lifebelts, no shelter, no nothing.

"We had no licence. Any licence you could have got just said 'for fresh water'. It didn't mention Lough Neagh and they maintained that that was no good when you went to court. That's where they had us. They wanted us to take out licences for the lough, but we would have had to sell any eels we caught to them at their price. I mean the people who claimed they owned the lough.

"They had patrol boats and if they caught us they lifted our lines and maybe sometimes summoned us as well. That is, if they were able to prove who laid the lines. They had to see us at it. We weren't so easy seen. When the patrol boat was first sighted somebody on the look-out would have put up a smokescreen. The smokescreen for this side was nearly always put up on Derryclone Point. It could be seen all over the shore. Usually they set fire to whins. Nothing burns as well as a whin bush and if it is green there's plenty of smoke.

"The Ardboe boys could see our smokescreen and lift their lines before Gibson got near them. That was what you called the man on the patrol boat. If the Ardboe boys spotted the patrol before our smokescreen went up, they put up a smokescreen first. Very often we just had time to get off the lough and lose our lines.

"The patrol boat put out a grab and pulled in the lines, moving at a slow speed. Any fish on them were thrown back. They didn't take the eels, just the lines. If they cut across your line when they were pulling in mine, they just tied floats to yours and came back and lifted it when they had finished with mine. They gathered up all the lines. That was what was going on all summer. Duff of Coagh was the main man. He gave out the licences and Gibson was one of his men. When you were summoned you had to go to Court, pay the fine and costs, and lose your line as well.

"There were pollan and other fish too. It was only the eels that they were after. The pollan weren't a good shipper. They were too soft and were mostly sold around the doors. There was one woman from Derryclone and she hawked fish far and wide on a bicycle, mostly in winter. 'Travelling Mary' or 'the traveller' they called her. The open season was from the 1st February until 31st October – but there were some fish caught in the close season and hawked around after dark to safe houses.

"The bailiffs didn't come on until the 1920s. I think that the Stormont Government was responsible. They were making changes. The patrol boat harboured down at Antrim all the time and they would have been up here before we got the lines lifted in the morning. There was some mornings they were early but some mornings they weren't so early. If they seen where you were – well, you had to go. If they got you they took your name and all. They got a hold of your line and took it forby. Sometimes when tempers were riz the police had to be sent for. They lifted our lines for thirty or forty years till they got the thing settled. A priest from Toomebridge got a Co-operative set up.

"There's very little fish or fishing on the lough now. Maybe it is because the water is so bad.

"I mind one time being in a barber's shop. Paddy Marley had a barber's shop down Castle Lane and a fine barber he was. The talk came round about Lough Neagh fish and we were arguing about eels. Paddy said to me.

'Did you see many eels in your day?' I said, 'I saw a brave lock' (lot). He said 'You didn't see as many as me.' He had been in the first war and that was where he learned the barbering. There was none better. Every morning he said we had to go to Billingsgate market for the army, for fish with a whole string of lorries. 'We were buying for the army, and nobody else got buying till we got our complement. Whatever we wanted,' and he said: 'What?' says he, 'did they buy the eels in Billingsgate market in the first war?' and I says 'Paddy, I don't know. I suppose a brave penny. I don't know!' 'Well,' he says, 'I know. I was there. I was with the army every morning. We were first. Nobody got buying so long as we were buying. We bought them,' he said, 'we bought the eels in Billingsgate market for 170 shillings a stone. I was there every morning.'

"Now he told us that, and Paddy Marley wouldn't have told a lie to nobody, and he said, 'And anybody that was there then could tell you the very same story.'"

There was somebody profiteering somewhere.

A picture of James Edward McAlinden's house at Derrymore taken in the early nineteen thirties. James Edw. had a small shop. He also shipped and merchanted all the eels caught locally. From left Pat Dorrian, Hugh Doon, A. N. Other.

Jimmy Matchett's Story

Jimmy Matchett, a retired carrier who has never ventured far from the Cairn, Aghalee, where he was born, has also given a graphic account of the bad old days. Jimmy is also in his mid-eighties.

"I went to school a while before the first war but not for very long and I didn't go every day. I left when I was 13. The school is there yet but it's a dwelling house now, beside Sherrin's Bridge. There were about 60 at it, boys and girls. There was a passageway down the middle with girls on the right and boys on the left – all barefooted.

"I loved going errands when I was young. Most people would have given you something for going. Very often it would only have been buttered bread with sugar sprinkled over it – no jam. Oul Barney McCrory used to roast a big spud and put salt and pepper on it for seasoning. He lived beside us and I got one regularly. They were lovely. Barney did handloom weaving and sometimes I would have got a penny for putting the threads through the wee holes in the loom for him. My eyes were better than his. William, John and Maggie McCorry were weavers as well and Margaret Hewitt of the Folly Hill.

"When the weavers had their cut finished they used to set off to Lurgan walking with the cut on their shoulder. They might have got a lift sometimes in a cart or a van if a farmer overtook them. Usually they set off at about ten o'clock without a bite in their bellies. They had five miles to walk. Coming back they would have had a bag of bobbins, the yarn. Mostly they went to a place 'up blough' in Lurgan – Ireland Bros., I think it was.

"I mind one day I had to go to Usher's pub on the Hollow Road where Patsy Tallon lives now. Some of the men who were working in a hayfield sent me for a quart of beer. They gave me sixpence (2^1/2p). I was heart-scared that I would lose it. I was only a wee lad and I was scared I would forget what I had to get. I ran like hell rhyming 'a quart of beer – a quart of beer – a quart of beer'. Dan Tallon who lived beside Ushers heard me and every time he saw me for a good while, he called me 'quart of beer'. I hated it.

"Usher was a 'quare oul codger' – he lived by himself and he only ate once a day. He kept five or six hens and he ate all their eggs every day, whether it was one or six.

"When I was at school I always had to hurry home to gather sticks or maybe to go to the moss (peat bog) for turf with the donkey and cart. When I started school first we had to bring a turf for the fire in the wintertime. There was only one fire for the whole school and we needed a big lot of turf to throw out any heat. There was no coal burned. There was no water in the school. We had to go across the road to Thomas John Bell's for drinks. Mrs. Bell cleaned the school.

Big James (1878 – 1957)

'Big James' Mulholland (1878 – 1957), who broke the mould of the traditional hearth industry on Lough Neagh's banks just prior to World War One when he hired men to hand-craft baskets in a factory and eventually provided constant insurable employment for over 30 men for some 30 years. (From a family portrait.)

What manner of man was James and what was his background? Those who were closest to him say, 'He was always a bit of a chancer'. They use the term with affection and admiration rather than in a derogatory sense. Obviously he had initiative, sound business acumen and a determination to succeed.

He was a very big man, so big that he was known locally as 'Big James', 'Big Mulholland' or 'the Osier Mulholland' to distinguish him from smaller neighbours of the same name. He looked a gentle giant and generally he did not get over-excited, but he was a strong character with a sharp intellect and the best pair of hands in the craft. They were oversized through hard usage but tradition has it that no one was ever able to match his dexterity in weaving osiers, trimming components and putting a shine on the finished product. Sometimes he would have playfully challenged a worker to complete a potato basket handle faster and generally he had two handles on before the other man had finished one. They say he handled an oversized knife like a scalpel.

He sprang from a family of seasonal fishermen and basket-makers, and is reputed to have loved fishing. On the lough he would have learned how to live by his wits for there was a constant battle there with the Fishery Inspector, as John McAlinden has told us. Fires were lit regularly at

were up nearly all night to get them done. My mother would have had to dry her coat at the fire when she got wet coming home. She hadn't any changes. She had a hard time and she didn't live to be an old woman.

"We had only a wee cottier house of Elliott's at first. There was no room at all. Then we had one of Turtle's. It was a bit bigger.

"Eventually we got a good big council cottage. It had three bedrooms and a big shop for four looms which made more room. We had no looms. The childer had to be washed of a Saturday night in a wooden tub in front of the fire. Sometimes mother did folding. She had a machine and she folded handkerchiefs for Campbell's of the Milltown. They got them from some of the factories.

"I stayed at Turtle's for 17 years. Some of them had died then and they went out of the milk business. Newsam took it over. The business in Belfast went as well. When I went to live in with a music teacher in Lurgan, called Smyth. I got two evenings a week off there. Later on I wrought for various people, mostly on a daily arrangement.

"I never got to dances or anything like that when I was young. They say what you never had you never miss. I never was used to nights off or going with boys. I had too hard to work."

1990 display of baskets by The Hannon Bros of Moss Rd Aghagallon. Photo P. Smyth

husband had been poisoned, or something, in a well. He had been a well sinker and he had gone down a well at Kirk's of Derryclone that had foul air in it. Her mother was doting and needed a lot of looking after so she had to get Jane for help. It wasn't a pub where men went and sat drinking. It was more a place where they bought a drop and went on.

"When Jane got work I had to stay at home to look after the wee ones. The wee ones couldn't be left on their own. My mother lost one. She went too near the fire and her wee nightie caught fire. They took her to the hospital but she died of shock. I cried for weeks about her.

"Then I got a job at Turtle's. They had a big dairy farm with 50 cows, beside us, and a shirt and blouse factory and a shop in Belfast. There were three men and two ladies. The men only come home of a Saturday and went away early on Monday morning, or Sunday night. The Misses Turtle ran the farm with the help of paid men. I had done wee errands for them and in and out from I was a wee girl. Then I got a full-time job. I wouldn't have been very old, maybe 13. It was very near home but I didn't get much time off – after tea on Wednesdays and on Sunday afternoons. I can't mind what I got. A lock (few) half-crowns, seven and six at first, I think, and later ten shillings (50p). That was by the month. I got my keep. They were very good to me. They always gave me a blouse at Christmas.

"I had to rise at five o'clock. The milk had to be at Lurgan Station at half-seven. My father had got a job at Turtle's before I started. He took the milk three miles to the station in kegs and he also delivered around the town. A few wee boys met him every morning and ran round the doors. People had their own can and things. The milkman measured it out for each customer – half-pints, pints and that sort of thing … a pen'ith (pennyworth) here and a ha'pith (half-penny worth) there.

"I lit fires, milked cows, washed and scalded milk vessels and did all sorts of jobs from five in the morning, before I got a bite to eat. Through the day I was always kept busy as well, although the ladies did the cooking and baking. In the evenings there was always brasses to clean and things like that. The ladies retired into the sitting room. There was always eggs to wash or something. They sold eggs and milk in the Belfast shop.

"I had hard to work but not as hard as my mother. At first she had to be in the factory at six o'clock in the morning and she had three miles to walk. Then it wore on that she hadn't to start until eight. When she was pregnant or just after having a baby it was very hard standing on her feet all day at a winding machine and walking to work and back. When she got home at night we would have had potatoes boiled, but after she had had a bite to eat she would have had two or three griddles of bread to bake. Then there was the thread-drawing. Some days we might have got 16 dozen handkerchiefs to be ready the next day. Mother drew out the first threads and then we drawed the doubles. We got three ha'pence a dozen (£1/160th). Sometimes we

"My mother kept two pigs. When they were fat Isaac Magee used to come and kill them. They were hung up by the heels for a day. My father took them to Daly's pork shop in North Street. Maybe, to Lurgan pork market and then to Daly's. I'm not sure. He would have brought two wee suckie (suckling) pigs home. When the pigs were sold we would have got boots and things for the winter. We went barefooted most of the time.

"My father bought a donkey and cart at one time off Dan Swainey (Sweeney) a dealer. Dan went on a spree to the Milltown pub, beside our house and then he came and took the donkey and cart back to get to Downing's pub at Derryhirk (a couple of miles distant). My father went after him for he had paid for the donkey. There was a row at Derryhirk but my father brought back the donkey.

"I didn't get much schooling; just a day now and again. Somebody had to stay at home to look after the childer and put on the dinner for my mother in the evening, and do wee turns. I did get about nine months at Derryclone school and I got on very well there. I was as good as any of them in the class when I had to leave. A woman in Derryclone called Rosie McKenna, was afraid to stay by herself when her daughter went to America, and left her on her own. The daughter didn't like America and she came home after nine months. Rosie was a great friend of my mother's and she had coaxed her to let me go and stay a wee while. As my mother had a houseful (the house was very small) she let me go. I didn't object as Rosie was very kind and I got a chance to go to school every day. She was very good to me and I was sorry to leave.

"Rosie was a midwife. In them days women having a child wouldn't have got any doctor. The midwife did everything. I mind she would have had to go out sometimes in the middle of the night. Whoever come for her would just have tinkled the window. That wakened me, I mind watching her putting on her big white apron. At other times I watched her fixing the folds in the front of the wee white cap that she had. She put tucks in it with the smoothing iron. She walked for miles at all hours. Of course, whoever come for her would have been there too. They had no bicycles or anything. Some of the men might have come with a pony or horse in a trap or a springcart maybe even with a donkey and cart. She thought nothing of walking as far as Lurgan. She went over the canal at the Gut (Ellis Gut).

"When she was away, I had to kindle the fire and make myself a drop of tea for my breakfast. It wasn't hard to light. The greeschia would have been red and covered up with a turf. I just put a dry sod (peat) on and it soon kindled. I wasn't a bit afraid about being left by myself at night. Nobody would have bothered with you in them days.

"Rosie and I used to gather rushes. She used them to make rush bottomed chairs.

"I wasn't long home until Jane got a job with Jinny Bunting. She had a public house on Kilmore Hill. Her first

The Thread-Drawer's Story

Three men have now given their recollections of social conditions on Lough Neagh's banks at the time James Mulholland decided to set up a basket factory. To complete the picture let us now hear Nellie Heaney's story. Nellie was the second eldest of a family of 11 whose father was a farm labourer and whose mother had to walk over three miles to the nearest textile factory to earn a little to supplement her husband's meagre earnings.

Ellen was born around the same time as Alfred Grant and James Matchett but she lived at Annaghdrougal near Ellis' Cut, for a time she lodged at Derryclone.

"I was born in 1905 – I think. I'm not rightly sure. There was 11 in the family. I wasn't the oldest: Jane was. My father did different things. He was ploughman for Tommy Elliott and later he was a milk roundsman at Turtle's. My mother was a winder in the Limited factory – the Blackstaff I think owned it. She had to get up about half past four. She had to light the fire and make a cup of tea before she started. It would have taken her more than an hour walking in. There were no buses or anything in those days. She had to be in for six o'clock in those days. In the dark mornings she was afraid to go by herself and my father used to walk with her to Taylor's turn.

"All she got was a cup of tea at dinnertime in the factory in what they called the 'cook house'. She would have had a piece with her and that was all they got then till they came home. It would have been between six and seven when she got home.

"We drawed handkerchiefs in the house as well. My mother, when we were very young, she took out the first thread. We did what was called the doubles; that was drawing the next two threads out. We all helped except Jane. Her eyesight wasn't so good and she did housework.

"My father was working in them days at Elliott's. I think he had about ten shillings (50p) a week and a free house – a wee house down at Droughal bridge. We got our milk at Elliott's and butter when they churned. We had to pay for them. You would have got a pen'ith of milk and a pen'ith of buttermilk. That is how they were sold. We got a can of buttermilk and a couple of pounds of butter every time they churned. They made lovely butter, country butter.

"I mind we all had to get vaccinated. My father got us all into the cart. He borrowed Elliott's horse and cart and he took us to Doctor Brownrigg's of Moira. He was our doctor as Droughal was in County Down. We were all taken into the doctor's and we got our arms done. He gave us wee pink sweets to keep us from crying. Mary was thrawn and cried a good deal. He called her 'Mary, Mary, quite contrary'. Then we all had sore arms together.

"Before I was very big I got taking the donkey and cart to Lurgan. Nearly every house had a pig and I would have had to take a pork pig to the market, which was beside the big church in Lurgan. I had to start about 7 o'clock in the morning to get there before the market opened at 9 o'clock. Carts were numbered as they arrived and when the town clock struck nine the market opened officially. You didn't get your ticket till nine, no matter how early you were. As soon as people got their tickets they took off for the weigh-bridge at Clay Town, down at the courthouse. It was like the Derby going down William Street: who could get to the weigh-bridge first with their cart.

"The buyer paid out when the banks opened at 10 o'clock. He paid out in the pub at the head of Carnegie Street, facing the Northern Bank. When they got paid some of the people who had got money went to an eating-house, Debbie Walker's at the back of the church or maybe McStravick's down the Pound River (that's what they called Edward Street) They got tea and beef for a shilling (5p). Sometimes they got a wee suckie pig before they went home. They had to pay the butcher Isaac Magee or Dick Magee – and they hadn't so much over by the time they got home, especially if they went for a bottle or two.

"If I had room in the cart sometimes I would have called at Heaney's of Killaghey on my way home for a ten-stone bag of hand-picked coal. The Cairn folk liked big coal from Heaney's. It cost eight shillings (40p) a quarter ton. I would have got 6d (2½p) for carting it home. Sometimes I would have had to bring a table or chair from one of the auction rooms in Lurgan.

"My father was a ploughman for Best. He had about twelve shillings a week (60p) but no mate (food). Best owned our house and it was rent free. My mother did whitework, stitching and thread-drawing of handkerchiefs, for some of the factories. She only got a few pence a dozen. There was no money anywhere but everybody was in the same boat. The herring men did a good trade. We always had salt herrings hanging up. The only time people got beef was when they sold a pork pig or something."

We will meet Jimmy again later on.

the Battery on the Tyrone shore to alert the Derrymore folk when the Inspector was on the lough, and Lough Neagh fishermen were quick to scarper when necessity arose.

'Big James's' parents were in the trade of making potato baskets on the hearth and marketing them themselves. Both of them attended markets as far afield as Dromore, County Down – 12 miles distant using a pony or a donkey for transport. His mother is said to have gone along to make sure that the money wasn't spent by her husband before he got it home. Traditionally, any yeast hampers which they had made had been sold to Judge, the Belfast merchant.

John McAlinden is one of the few people still living who can recall the time that James Mulholland took the plunge. John was a school boy at the time and he avers that the man from the distillery was quite lost when he got to Derryhirk and didn't know exactly who he had come to look for. McAlister's pub was at Derryhirk which may have caused the agent to become a bit confused. At least, that has been hinted at.

Here is John's account:

"This man from Avoniel Distillery arrived at Derryhirk pub looking for a certain party to make a lot of yeast hampers. There's a lot of Laverys, McConaghys, O'Neills, McAlindens and Mulhollands round the bay (Bartin's) and the poor man wasn't sure which of them he had been told to go to. 'Big James' was there and when he heard the man's errand and the price he was prepared to pay, he jumped in.

A display of the three tools: secateurs, knife and borer used by the Mulholland brothers in 1990 to make a potato basket. Traditionally an ash peg was used as a borer when a metal one was not available.

'My name's James Mulholland and I make baskets,' he said. 'I'll make skips for you.'

"How he was going to do it probably hadn't entered his head. He was that kind of man. He saw his chance and he took it. Anyhow he got the order, a very big one, and then he had to get an old outhouse and a lot of boys (men) to help him. He had no money, nor anything but he wasn't going to be bate. He had been making for a Belfast concern, Judge's, up till then and so had his father and brothers, but James had his head screwed on and he wanted to cut out the middle man.

"Fortunately, very few tools were needed and rods were plentiful. There was also plenty of men looking for work. That's how it all started."

The Mulholland farmhouse at Gawley's Gate would have been a little bigger than the cottier houses nearby, as the family owned a few acres of the lough shore, but James Mulholland certainly was not born with a silver spoon in his mouth. Like most of his neighbours he would have known what poverty was. As a farm labourer, he could perhaps have earned two shillings a day (10p in modern money), with a meal provided, but when he decided to take a wife he needed more. For a time he carried on making baskets for Judge but, as already mentioned, at the first opportunity he decided to strike out on his own and got a few men to work for him.

Firstly, he got the tenancy of a wee cottier house at nearby Grant's Lane, then one belonging to a local farmer, O'Hara of Derrymore, where he made skeps and potato baskets. His wife helped there initially by bottoming baskets when her husband set up the framework. Then he moved to Derrymore but that house was so small that 'Big James' was driven to complain that, 'We cannot even get into it'.

Next he moved on to a place between Ballykeel (Fruit Hill) and Tamnavane which had the peculiar name 'Castle Dunk' but after a short stay there he was off again. This time to a place nearly opposite Derryhirk Inn, where O'Rawes had lived. Finally, and obviously with a bit of money made, he purchased a fine farm near Gilbert's Bridge on the Lurgan to Aghalee road (B12) from Stephen Gilbert. The dwelling house and out-offices were in a single row and thatched, but James hadn't been long in residence when they were gutted by a disastrous fire, in July. When rebuilding took place, he put up several workshops around the perimeter of the farmyard where he eventually assembled the largest workforce ever in the parish of Aghagallon.

During the First World War demand for yeast hampers was good and that was when James Mulholland made most money. Rods were cheap then – about fifteen shillings to £1 a ton. Much later Judge paid up to £20 a ton when competition from Mulholland left him short of supplies. When he was well established 'Big James' stockpiled tons of rods in huge thatched 'hovels' (stacks). They kept for years and only needed to be well steeped before use. His

Jack Mallon stacking skeps at Mulholland's of Gawley's Gate. Photograph from the Ulster Folk Museum Green Collection.

buffer stock would have given him the edge on his competitor and left him in a position to suspend buying until the price stabilised.

James married Annie O'Neill of Cornakinnegar, Lurgan and they had three sons and five daughters: James, Thomas, Dermot, Maureen, Kathleen, Rita, Dympna and Maeve. Thomas and Kathleen (Mrs. Moore) are now deceased.

His brothers, William and Thomas continued in the basket trade in the Gawley's Gate area after he set up at Aghagallon Road. William remained at the ancestral home and Thomas went into business at Derryola which is an adjoining townland. Their sons also carried on the trade in the succeeding generation, and at times some of his nephews worked with 'Big James' at his factory. Now (in 1991) a grandson of 'Big James', David Moore, is keeping the craft alive at Lurgan Road Aghagallon near Whitehall, as are his sons James and Dermot on an occasional basis.

Dermot Mulholland outside 'Big James' Mulholland's workshop in 1990. Photo: P. Smyth.

The Factory (Workshops)

James Mulholland's basket factory was located on the (B12) at a junction known as Stephen's Corner – named after Stephen Gilbert which is about three miles from Gawley's Gate and four from Lurgan. That corner had long been the traditional meeting place for local men. There would seldom have had been less than a dozen loitering there from seven or eight o'clock in the evening until bedtime in favourable weather. When the basket factory was set up some of these men drifted into the workshops for a ceili. The basket-makers didn't mind, being well able to talk and work and so long as production was not impeded 'Big James' wouldn't have minded a bit of crack. In the summer evenings he regularly joined the men assembled out-of-doors at Stephen's Corner.

Around Mulholland's yard, the low workshop, the meal house, the bullock shed and the upper workshop were all utilised for various purposes connected with basket-making – plus the boss's own wee workshop, nicknamed 'The Senate'. Although they were the élite of the workforce, men had to work in the low workshop when they were making potato baskets. The upper workshop was the better shop but only used for making 'skips' (yeast hampers).

Mulholland's workshops doubled as a kind of mini-community centre (for men only, of course.) 'Big James' had a small private workshop of his own, where a select few of the local sages assembled. One of these named Frank Carville, doyen of the group, dubbed it 'The Senate', and the name stuck. Presumably politics got regular airings. Frank was what was known locally as 'a long-headed old boy' – one of those rustic characters who always have an apt quip.

The initial workforce comprised seasonal fishermen, small holders, turfmakers and labourers. They would have been a very hardy breed accustomed to working out-of-doors in all weather and would have scorned the notion of sitting by a fire. A man who couldn't keep himself warm by working would quickly have been dubbed a 'cowl-rife cratur' locally. Sitting 'in the ashes' was 'an oul woman's place' and scorned by the menfolk. For that reason it was natural that in the early years the workshops were left unheated, but it is understandable that after a year or so of squatting in a cold shed for up to 12 hours a day working only with their hands, the men would have become 'cold-rife'.

Walking or cycling to and from work would have provided some exercise but not enough at least for the more elderly, new to a sedentary occupation – a very big change for them from following a pair of horses ploughing the day long, or working in a turf bog, or around a farmyard. Anyhow, open fires were eventually installed in the workshops. There were plenty of wood chippings for firing.

Since there was no public transport, all the workers had either to walk or cycle, but neither before nor since has any similar local enterprise provided constant work in the particular area for so many men. Usually the workforce was around the 30 mark and numbers remained steady over most of the period from the time of World War I until the outbreak of the 1939–45 War.

Paraffin-oil-fuelled lamps hung on the walls were used for illumination. The traditional style tin lamps with a double-burner (wick) and bright reflector were preferred. Each pair of workers shared a lamp, which they purchased jointly and kept supplied with oil. Occasionally a prankster would have stolen a worker's oil and substituted water – 'then maybe he would have had to pack up and go home because he had no light'.

Mulholland's men usually sat down to make baskets (or 'skips') around nine o'clock in the morning. I have been told that for many years eight of them clubbed together to buy an empty 'sweetie' can from the local shopkeeper. (Originally Dan O'Hara and later, Sam Watson). The can cost eight pence and Alfred Grant who took up the collection is adamant that he had difficulty in getting the penny contribution from some of the men. 'They just hadn't a ha'penny and the can might have been nearly wore out before I got it' he has remarked. Tea was brewed over a fire in this makeshift Billy can at about 12.30 p.m. daily. Each man put in a morsel of tea and brought 'a piece' (no food was provided) and that was the only tea-break even if they wrought to bedtime which was not unusual. 'A man might have snatched a bite of dry bread as he wrought, if he was very hungry.'

Average output was $2^1/2$ dozen 'skips' a day per man and the pay was 30 (old) pence ($12^1/2$p) a dozen. Wee John Mulholland (no relation of 'Big James') is remembered as the local champion who was able to make three dozen a day. One chap called 'Wee Paddy' was only able to make two dozen or less and he was such a heavy smoker that he smoked nearly all he earned. (Five 'Woodbine' cigarettes cost 2d (less than 1p) in those days). Some of the skip makers, about nine altogether were able to make potato baskets and they were switched by Big Jim when he needed them. They got five shillings and six pence a dozen for those and good basket-makers made about four and a half dozens in the $5^1/2$ day week, i.e. about 10 a day. Each held half a cwt. of potatoes. There were only two or three good basket-makers in the factory. The rest made about $3^1/2$ dozen, maybe four dozen.

From left: Joe Russell and a sister of 'Big James', either Mrs McNally or Mrs Lavery, i.e. Anne or Selina, at Gawley's Gate. Photograph from the Ulster Folk Museum Green Collection.

The Cultivation and Preparation of Raw Material

In his history of County Down published in 1875, Alexander Knox, M.D., identified the traditional basket-maker's willow osier as *salix viminalis*. It needs to be allowed to mature, hence harvesting usually takes place in winter, but in Mulholland's day there was what was called 'the green season' when some growers, especially if they were pushed for money, harvested their osiers around September. Baskets made from green unseasoned rods look very attractive but they are not durable. They are too heavy as well. Rods which have been allowed to mature naturally are best. Flooding the land or top dressing with farm-yard manure was tried by some growers to force growth but knowledgeable local men say that it was best not to force the rods but to let them mature naturally. Bushy specimens were inferior. Some wild osiers were used by thatchers. These grew profusely in the fen land. The Mulholland family still cultivate a small acreage of osiers for thatchers.

Very few of the men who made baskets in Mulholland's workshop are alive today. Octogenarian Alfred Grant of Brankinstown can still provide a vivid account of everything connected with the industry. Here is his verbatim account of the cultivation of osiers:

"... To grow osiers, ground had to be ploughed, maybe up to 15 inches deep. There was no rotovators in them days. It had to be harrowed, and clod-crushers would have been brought in to make it fine. It had to be done by the horses. There was a line put down the field. If the field was maybe, five acres, there might have been a line maybe, 300 yards long. You needed two lines actually, a double line, and you put them down that field. First, the field was rolled; it had to be rolled beforehand.

"You cut your sett, your plant, what they called 'a sett'. And it had to be 12 or 13, maybe 15 inches long. Cut with a good sharp knife (at an angle). You needed a good clean cut. You planted down the side of the line with the white showing on the sett as we call it. It had to be showing down that line to the east. The farmers liked it that way, or with the back to the north. The farmer, he thought they grew better when they were planted that way.

"They only planted 'willies'; the 'sallies' weren't so good. They were branchy. The osier was better than the sally. The sally was rough and branchy. But it was just like bringing new breeds in – the way they have done with cattle now. Everybody got smart and they grew their own stuff. There was a man called John McCartan of Deerpark. All his osiers were the double-eyed Irish rod. There was no such a thing hardly as breaking them. They went round the rim of the basket like silk. The skin, the bark, was like silk. If you grew them in moss ground they were no use. They only made yeast hampers but not potato baskets.

Johnny Barnes and an unknown man posing for a photographer at Gawley's Gate, circa 1930. They are demonstrating how bundles of rods were stacked and carried to the workshop. Photograph from the Ulster Folk Museum Green Collection.

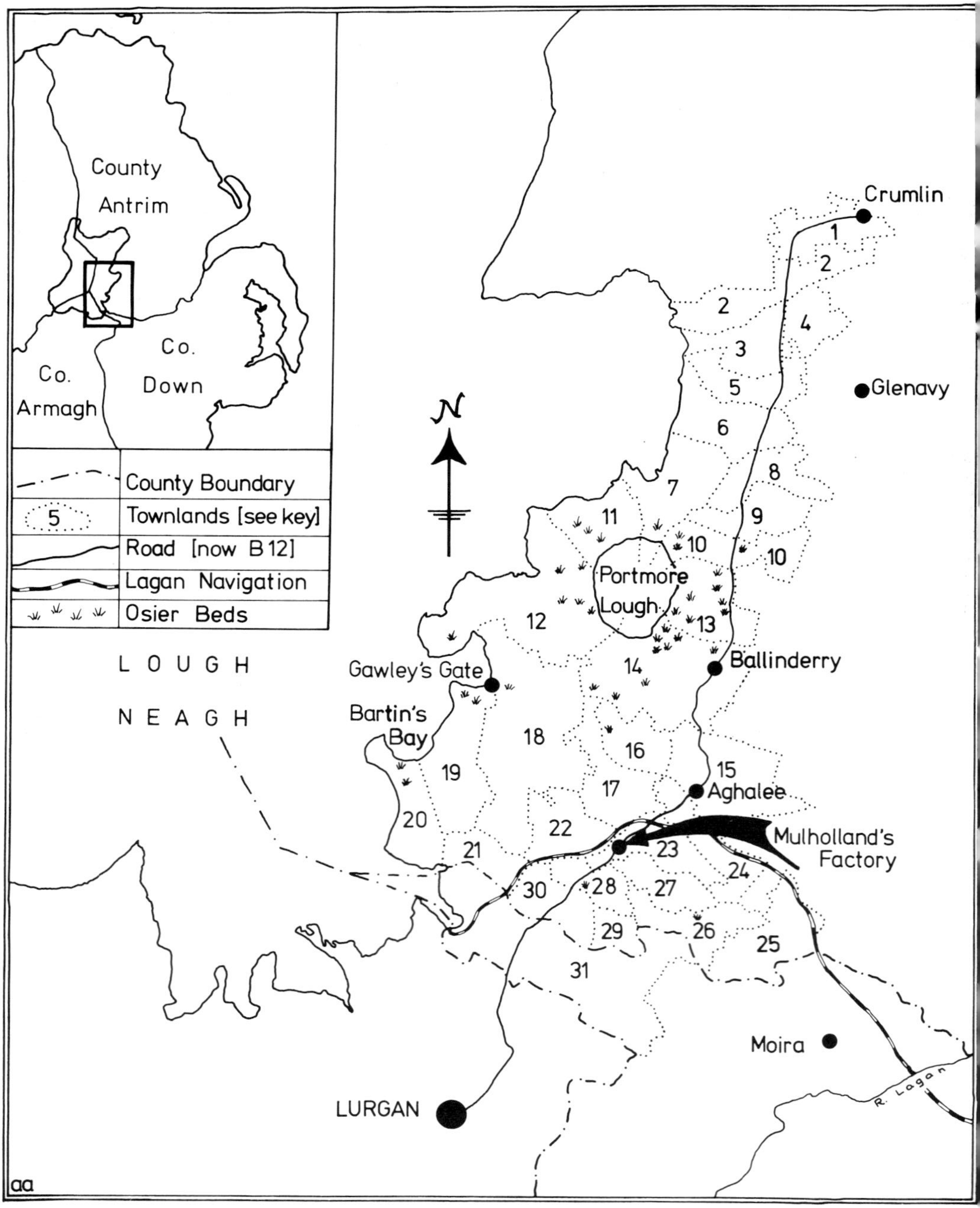
County Antrim
Co. Down
Co. Armagh
County Boundary
Townlands [see key]
Road [now B 12]
Lagan Navigation
Osier Beds
LOUGH NEAGH
Crumlin
Glenavy
Portmore Lough
Ballinderry
Gawley's Gate
Bartin's Bay
Aghalee
Mulholland's Factory
Moira
LURGAN
R. Lagan
1
2
2
3
4
5
6
7
8
9
10
10
11
12
13
14
15
16
17
18
19
20
21
22
23
24
25
26
27
28
29
30
31
aa

KEY TO MAP

ANCIENT MAP OF S. W. ANTRIM

1. BALLYTROMERY
2. BALLYSHANAGHILL
3. AGHNADARRAGH
4. LANGARVE
5. BALLYVOLLEN
6. BALLYVORALLY
7. BALLYVANEN
8. AGHADOLGAN
9. BALLYMACREVAN
10. LURGILL
11. FEUMORE
12. DEER PARK
13. PORTMORE
14. BALLINDERRY
15. AGHALEE
16. BALLYMACILRANY
17. BALLYCAIRN
18. MONTIAGHS
19. DERRYMORE
20. DERRYCLONE
21. DERRYHIRK
22. DRUMALEET
23. AGHAGALLON
24. KILLOUGH
25. POOBLES
26. AGHADRUMGLASNY
27. BALLYKEEL
28. DERRYNASEER
29. TAMNYVANE
30. TISCALLEN
31. KILMORE

From Knox's History of County Down, Hodges Foster & Co. Dublin (1875), Lough Money which Alfred Grant has referred to at page 10 is now but a swamp.

Never did ever I see anything like them. They are all away now.

"When a man was going to plant the rods he had them all in bundles and he drew them out with his hand from the top of a bundle. He drew maybe 15 or 16 of the top ones. They would have been anything from 12 to 15 inches long. That made the setts for putting in the ground. You wouldn't have put in a wee 'twangley' one because if you did, it didn't do the first year. It didn't develop the first year into anything of any use. Sometimes they did that; they set (planted) tops. They might have been 12 or 15 inches long and they put them in you see, in the rows and they didn't develop into anything. They took over at 'the sett' (i.e. the base) and might bring up two or three osiers at the one time.

"James Mulholland grew most of his own rods – fields full of them and he got the seed from McCartan. In fact, anybody that was getting McCartan's osiers was getting first-class material. He would have been paying dear for them, but you never would see one like them now.

"Labouring had to be done. I don't think what (implements) they have now would be any use to them. That wee 'sett' that I mentioned the wee fibres grow out across the bottom of the row. Well at that time that had all to be dug around with a spade to take the weeds out. There was a man – he is deceased now – Tommy McCavigan. He wrought for Mr. Mairs in 'the Park' (Deerpark): he dug eight acres to weed them. In fact, he dug eight acres of ground for the rods to be planted in first. There never was a spadesman like him in this part of the country. He died in 1989. Whenever you were digging to weed you had to take a wee chip out between the setts with the point of your spade and turn that up. And the next year they were dug again – two years they were dug (weeded) – and there was a woman in Brankinstown they called Rose Doone, and Rose got a contract at Mairs for weeding them rods, all the grass and weeds out of them. And she cleaned them eight acres of a winter's day, and she had nothing on her feet but a pair of gutty slippers. You can guess what that old soul had to suffer. And she was getting tuppence a row, and they were anything up to, maybe, 400 yards long. And the ground was wet. Yet she lived to a ripe old age. She lived to over 90. (And I'll tell you something. There's no place you'll die as quick, if you sit around the fire.)

"Harvesting was done generally about November. You had to have a special hook for cutting them – a scythe hook you called it, one with a back on it, a riveted back. It was a thin hook you could always have put a good edge on, but you needed a good sharpening stone. And it wasn't everybody could do that, either. Now that man, McCavigan, he was an expert at cutting too. There was a man they called James McKeveney, down in the Deerpark that lived beside Mairs and he said that whatever McCavigan was doing he always could beat it. And they were sitting at the fire this night in Mairs' and he said to Mr. Mairs, 'I'll handle McCavigan the morrow if I can. But I'll never work as hard again as I will the morrow, till I see what I can do with him'.

"So out they goes and McKeveney starts off and he's cutting away and he keeps a wee bit in front. And he's all pleased with himself, when they have only about 10 yards for to go out at the end (on to the headrig as they called it), and him still in front. And when he looked around what was McCavigan doing? He was coming behind but had two rows cut! So McKeveney said, 'I'll talk no more. I can cut no rods'. And he was getting so much a row for cutting.

"There was a stump left when you were cutting. And there was always a wee bit of a lean in that stump, and you had to get round that with your hook. You just couldn't have cut in just anywhere. You had to go round that stump and cut it off neatly. If you hadn't, you would have spoiled your sett for another year. Do you see?

"To tie up the rods after you had them cut and laid down in tiers where you put them, then you picked one good decent rod, laid it down and put your foot on it, holding the butt-end of it in your right hand. You put your finger about six inches from the top end, and bent the rod over, and twisted it into a loop. Then you laid the single rod down flat – you called it a withe – and laid the cut rods across it in a bundle. You put half a hundred weight in a bundle. You could have guessed it with your eye. Then you put the single end of the withe through the eye on the other end, put your foot on it and pulled it up tight and tucked the end in and twisted it so that it would not loosen. Sometimes they had to be carried out of the field because of wet weather, and at that time there was nothing for to draw them with only the horse and cart.

"It was a very awkward job too, for a man to build them. It took a man to know what he was doing for to build a load of rods on a cart.

"He had to tie … he had to put the butts to the horse's back and more butts to the back door of the cart and he kept a wee handful of rods and put it in for to catch the next bundle of rods going on for to tie it, or the whole thing would have fell over the wheel. A skill of its own.

"Them rods that I'm telling you about, that they cut, when it come to March, they go stale and 'gazined' as we called it – and they wouldn't bend so they had to be 'stept'. They were carried to the drain and 'stept' in the water, for about seven days. All according to their kind – you had to know how long – if you had good material it didn't take as long steeping them if you hadn't … James Mulholland bought rods in Dungannon one time. He got them somewhere beside a canal or something there and they were very bad material. They made yeast hampers but they wouldn't make baskets. He got some like them at Lisburn too, down at Hilden. In there at the back of Hilden mill, and they were the worst material that ever come to Aghagallon. We all hated to see them coming…

"Yeast baskets, locally termed 'skips,' were cheap, roughly-fashioned, one-trip articles and the rods (osiers) which were used were inferior in quality to those needed for making potato baskets, which had to be much more durable. The low-grade osiers used for weaving the skips, were referred to as 'slewin'. Mostly the 'slewin' was imported. It needed to be steeped in water for at least a week to make it pliable. A slow stream which crossed a field of Mulholland's farm near the workshop was used for steeping rods. Bundles for steeping were doled out to the workers in the farmyard by 'Big James' personally, to preserve the peace. This was called 'getting your steep' by the workers. (They queued up to get their allocation.) The rods were tightly-bound together, with all the butts at one end, in bundles which weighed about 56 lbs. Some of the slewin was more bushy (branchy) than the rest.

"Workers carried bundles of dry rods three at a time to the river piled on one shoulder. Each watched his own like a hawk, carefully marking where he put them, and each had his own spot in the river. No worker would have dared to touch a mate's 'steep'. Each would have steeped maybe, 20 bundles (enough for a week's work). After a week when they were due to be retrieved, the worker took them out one at a time, stood the bundle on its butt-end on the brow of the river to drain, and then 'humped' them back to the workshop. One wet bundle was all any man could carry. He used only one at a time anyhow. Often they would have been dreeping down your back as you carried them. In heavy frost it was a-tarra. There would have been icicles on them half-a-foot long and they wouldn't steep right at all in bad frost. There wasn't much steeping done with rods for baskets. It was mostly the foreign rods for skips that had to be steeped.

"When you got to Mulholland's in the morning, the first thing you done was bring in two bundles of rods. Before you started you picked them rods. You took out the fine ones and all the wee stuff, and the branchy ones for 'skips'. The next thing you done was to cut your rods for the rims. You needed two rods for each basket and you would have cut enough for about 10 baskets. When you had that done, you got your rib timber. Maybe, you would have had some fir split. If not you had to cleave it with the hatchet and pare it. You would have made maybe 36 ribs all the breadth of your two fingers, thin enough to bend nicely but not break. You shaved them with a sharp knife, every one the same. With the two bundles of rods that you had picked you would have had what would have made you 10 baskets. The stuff was wet and maybe there was ice on it. It was a cold start but we were used to it and thought nothing of it. A bit of crack helped."

For years Mulholland imported ready-made rims or hoops for potato baskets from Holland and the 'slewin' or low grade osiers for yeast hampers, from Somerset. Fir timber for ribs was got from locally grown she fir trees which 'Big James' felled and carted home for conversion.

In a conversation which I had with Alfred Grant he gave me his recollections of the origin and fashioning of the various components. Here it is in his own words:

"The word 'slewin' was used for the rods which were got to weave skips. The word 'skimming' was used for the way of sorting the slewin by fingering it over at the weaving stage. (A groping action with outspread fingers and the palm of the right hand upwards was used to mime the craftsmanship at this stage.)

"Imported 'slewin' came by Belfast harbour and by rail to Lurgan where Hughie McCreanor collected them with a horse-drawn cart.

"'Slewin' came from Somerset and from the Low Countries, neatly packed in 3 foot, 4 foot and 5 foot bundles, 'all matched, not a rod out of place'. By skimming slewin carefully a skip maker could have saved his boss a lot of money. Jimmy Cinnamond (from the Islands) was the local expert. The dross from rods used for baskets also did for skips. Rods used for stakes (posts) had to be notched at the bends. To weave the wicker work over one stake and under the next an uneven number of stakes (posts) were essential or you would have went off your slew. Side stakes or posts were called 'scallems'. They were mostly home grown rods but some came from across the water. Originally the hoops were grew in Holland. They were to make the rim of the basket. Well, now the Dutch grew them rods for so many years – as far as I am informed from three to four years, and they were split by some sort of a machine and they used to make hoops for barrels too. And they were tied up in two dozen and one, and you never saw anything like the way they put them up in Holland. You talk about tradesmanship. It was something what I never forgot. I'll tell you. The way that they were put up, they were put up in a tight hoop, and there was like a wee loop of a rod tied round each hoop and that two-dozen-and-one in the coil (they called it) was lapped with an osier and twisted and put in. It took you to have a pair of snappers to open them. You never seen anything that was put up like them. They were as tight.... James Mulholland would have brought them home from the docks in Belfast and they would have been sitting up maybe 10 or 12 rows high and there never was the one – I never remember even one bursting. It was something I will always remember. They were used for the rims of the basket. Each one was a rod split in two, like what are used on apple barrels for hoops.

"You needed fir for the white ribs for the centre of the basket. And you got timber for ribs from farmers in this part of the country. James Mulholland flitted Tommy Hayes from Killyman. He used to get fir trees from Dungannon or sometimes Coalisland. When Mr. Hayes came from Killyman to Broomount (formerly owned by Stafford Gorman), he shifted him with his lorry and him and him got very great. And at Broomount estate every other tree in the plantin' in front of Soldierstown church was a fir when Hayes bought the place about 1925. Mulholland got them for making ribs.

"When the ribs couldn't be got any longer from Holland or anywhere else we were in a fix, but we sat down and worked it out. I had a hand in making the first rim from two big rods that had been grown locally. 'The Big Fellow' and I worked at it a long time but we got it right in the end."

Chippings and other residual material provided very acceptable firewood for poor families in the factory locality. These included the workers' families. One poor lady who had only five shillings a week outdoor relief from the Poor Law Guardians to live on was a regular scavenger for firewood. The workers would have tossed a bit of good fir to her on occasions, or she might have picked some up herself. Cubs from the neighbourhood did likewise, taking more liberties when the boss was away than when he was around. When heavy inroads were made in good fir timber, 'Big James' used to make what one of the cubs now calls a 'Commando raid'. (The cub is now past seventy!)

'Big James' residence and the workshops beyond. Taken from Gilbert's Bridge (Bl2) in 1990. Photo: P. Smyth.

Osiers for Shipyard

Thomas Barnes of Lower Ballinderry, another octogenarian, whose father worked for Thomas Creaney of George's Island (near Deerpark) also has vivid recollections of how osiers for Queen's Island were cultivated and marketed, when he was a boy. He recalls that Creaney had one 10-acre field, another of about nine acres, half of another field (about five acres, and a fourth plot of four or five acres, all planted with rods – about 30 acres altogether. At one time he harvested one-year-old osiers for the basket trade, some of the normal kind and some of the very fine variety used as withes. In addition, he let some osiers grow for two years before harvesting them. These were for sale to Belfast shipyard who needed coarse rods for tool holders.

Those for Queen's Island were cut in three-foot lengths and packed in bundles of 100. The osiers were laid flat on a bench in handfuls of three, butted against an endstop and chopped off at a three-foot mark on the bench, with a tool like a butcher's cleaver. Then the men laid them down (still in threes) and when they got thirty-three of these they added one to make up the 100 and bound them securely with fine rods (withes).

Two big loads on a cart fitted with wings, and high sides went at a time to the shipyard sometimes twice a year. Tom Barnes, Senior, and Bob Laird of Ballinderry were the carters. Creaney brought presents of tobacco and other things to the men in the shipyard as 'sweeteners'. In response, they refused to use any rods except Creaney's. They steamed the thick osiers and twisted some together to form a holder for a metal cutting tool, a kind of oversize cold chisel. When they twisted the osiers together they left a loop, or an eye, at one end into which the chisel was inserted. It wasn't a tight fit. The chisel was struck with a sledgehammer used to cut metal. The osier handle absorbed all the vibration. A solid handle would have been no good.

Harry Addis, who was a process server, and Bunting Thompson, wrought for Creaney. Lighter grade rods were sold to Campbell of the Bog Head, Totten's of Moss Lane, and other local basket-makers. Thomas Creaney died fairly young and Mrs. Creaney (née Annie Morrow) carried on the farming.

According to Thomas Barnes, setts were cut about nine inches long or longer and planted deep in the soil. "A line was used in planting. The setts would have been spaced about $1^1/2$ feet apart and the rows were about $2^1/2$ feet from one another. When you were cutting rods you always went to the sheltered side. They were nine or ten feet tall and great shelter. Old stumps got crooked and gnarled and had to be stubbed with a mattock. Then the ground was ploughed and cultivated before new setts were planted. The old stumps make great firewood. Ploughing ground where rods had grown was very heavy work for horses. Tractors were a fine improvement when they came." Tom recalls that men on a farm got 10/- (50p) a week and some mate (food). "I mind one man left the place he was at when he was offered 11/- (55p) a week elsewhere. A shilling (5p) was big money in my young days. I had to work for six shillings (30p) when I was 16 and I had to go seven days a week, and *no* mate (food). I had to take a piece." (That would have been around 1920.)

Weighbridge used for weighing rods (and coal) by "Big James". Photo P. Smyth 1990

Potato baskets stacked, probably on Willie Mulholland's farm at Gawley's Gate, where 'Big James' was born. Circa 1930. Photograph from the Ulster Folk Museum Green Collection.

43

The Baskets

The traditional wicker potato basket was a thing of beauty, well-designed and beautifully made. As a log basket or a clothes basket it would have fitted in with the best of indoor furnishings. In its intended role as a potato basket it was destined to be thrown down in muddy potato plots, pushed around by equally muddy hobnailed boots, and banged off the wooden wings of farm carts. It always looked far too good, and smelled too nicely for such rough treatment. The high quality material which went into it meant that it lasted for years, if given any kind of decent care. Mulholland always like to see a wet harvest season. More mud stuck to the baskets in the field and the heavier they got the more trailing around they received, wearing out the bases.

The humble yeast hamper was out of a different stable – sort of rectangular, poorly constructed and generally shapeless. One trip was all that it had to make and the men who put them together did not concern themselves with how they looked. Overall dimensions were 20 inches long, 18 wide and 13 deep. Approximately twelve stout rods, called 'scallems' were cut to size for use as upright posts, then six stakes for each end, and five bottom sticks. Handfuls of second-grade osiers were slewed around the posts and around the bottom sticks, and the skip was hurriedly thrown together on a base-board.

Basketmakers mare which was used by the McAreavey family of Aghadalgon, Glenavy, and is now in the possession of Gerard McAreavey. Photo: P. Smyth.

Each man used a purpose-made base-board about two feet by three feet which he positioned between his legs, steadying it with his knees. The board carried two slats of 3" x 3" timber, and there had to be a divide in it to catch the bottom sticks of the hamper.

The base-board was used to keep the frame in place initially. It didn't take long to make a skip and the rate of pay was correspondingly poor. At a later stage 'Big James' brought in a modification using dividers, the better to accommodate four bags (packets) of yeast.

Basket-makers used various knives. They had their own preferences. Some used a shoemaker's type, some 'a pig sticker's', others a big butcher's knife. 'Big James' had one of the latter. He was a very strong man with powerful wrists and very deft even with the big knife.

When making potato baskets, the higher skilled men who did both moved to Mulholland's low workshop where they sat on wooden boxes (crates). In addition to a sharp knife and snappers they needed various other implements, starting with a good sharp hand-hatchet for splitting blocks of fir timber into ribs. The fir block had to be split in two, quartered, etc. until it was a suitable thickness. Blocks were first sawn off tree trunks in $2^1/2$ foot lengths. A 'lot knife' was used to pare the ribs to size. They were placed on a purpose-made support fashioned from a fork of an ash bough and called 'a horse'. This was shaped like a giant catapult. They nailed two slats of wood to the obverse and another on the reverse. These horses were balanced on the men's knees and used to clamp the piece of wood being shaped. The lot knife was fashioned from a blacksmith's worn-out flatfile. It hadn't to be too sharp or too blunt. One end was turned

Potato basket: rim, cage and finished item. Three stages of making a traditional potato basket demonstrated by Dermot Mulholland, youngest son of 'Big James' of Aghagallon. Photo: P. Smyth, 1990.

round to make a holder for a wooden handle. The handle went in at right angles giving the knife an 'L' shape. Sam Greer, whose smithy was close by, made lot knives.

Another old-time knife called 'a drawing knife' was used at one time for shaving ribs, 'but you needed a frame for your feet while using it'.* The one around Mulholland's workshop was said to have been maybe up to 150 years old. It has since been mislaid. (*This was probably 'a mare' – see page 44.)

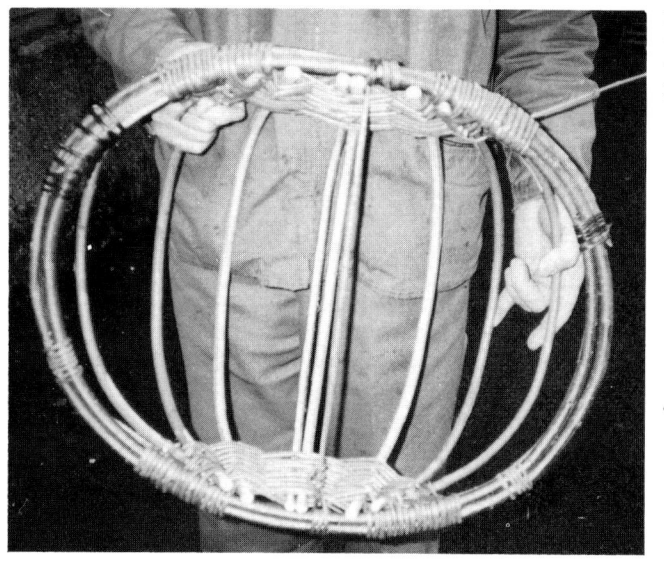

Ribs had to be pared down until they were the minimum thickness consistent with the strength needed. They were 2½ inches wide and maybe, one-eighth inch thick, when finished – pliable but tough and unbreakable.

"You would always have recognised a basket-maker by the knees of his trousers, worn in holes or patched, some with the odd slit in them. Men wore neither aprons nor gloves and some got boils on their bums. One man had to go to Dr. Deeny of Lurgan and get such a boil lanced. When he came back to the workshop he cut a round hole in the wooden box that he sat on, to save the wound, and wrought on. There was no workmen's compensation or National Health Service – just poverty", is how one ex-basket-maker has put it.

Rim and rib cage of potato basket specially made for the author's inspection by Dermot Mulholland. Since this type of basket no longer has to stand rough handling, fir ribs are no longer inserted. The baskets are used nowadays for artistic/ornamental purposes.
Photo: P. Smyth, 1990.

Setting Up

The art of setting up a basket, i.e. fashioning the framework has been described to me as follows:

"First of all, you must trim the rods for making the rim and take 'a skelp' out of the ends of them with a knife where they are to join. When you have to wrap the joint with a fine rod, a withe. From the elbow to the tip of the middle finger was the usual measure for the hoop (rim), about 20 inches. Next, you put what we call 'a bridle' across that hoop to pull it into a kind of oval shape.

"Next, you put in one white rib on the left hand side, and two white ribs on the right hand side and wrap a couple of withes round their ends to keep them in their places. The ribs have to be measured and taken across the basket, then fastened to the rims of the basket on the opposite side. An experienced man can tell with his eye what length of ribs he needs to give the basket the right depth.

"Next, you cut two osiers and put them in as green ribs alongside the white ones. These are called the fourth rib. Wrap a couple of fine osiers round them, too, to held them in place on the rim. That gives you five ribs altogether. When you put in two more green ribs again, two on either side of the white ones. That gives you nine altogether. You need an odd number to slew.

"When you weave a basket you start at the shoulder and grade the rods to taper the thickness of the sides, stronger at the top than lower down, but when you are within four inches of the centre of the bottom you begin to use thicker rods to give strength. A potato basket needs a flat bottom. Amateurs very often spoil them with a rounded bottom. When they rock and are too easily 'cowped' (overturned).

"A good basket is as tight as a drum, with all the rod ends neatly trimmed off with a sharp knife. A well made basket will stand an awful lot of knocks and with a bit of care last for years."

Fir timber is no longer used for ribs; instead strong rods are substituted.

Transport

'Big James' despatched and received goods by rail in the days when he had only horse-drawn vehicles. Hugh McCreanor, who has already been mentioned, was his horseman and he delivered finished products to the local GNR station at Lurgan with a mare and cart and also collected imported 'slewins', hoops and other kinds of rods. Ponies were used for transport in the very early years. The station was about four miles distant from the Stephen's Corner factory.

As soon as they became available in the early 1920s, Mulholland got a motor vehicle. His first was a Model T Ford saloon which he converted for the carriage of goods. Later, he got a Karrier. He bought the tractor only, and a local carpenter, Dick Magee, constructed the body which was an over-sized contraption of light construction. 'Big James' who by then had begun to sell coal, had to avoid overloading it with coal 'or it would have broken in two'. These early motor vehicles had, of course, solid tyres. Tradition has it that a local shop assistant, Tommy Cairns once got a lift to Belfast on the Karrier and afterwards complained that he had blisters on his bum when he got there.

When Dick Magee constructed the cabins of Mulholland's early goods vehicles, he only put one door in them. Once, when 'Big James' got his lorry bogged down in a soft verge on Rocklane near home and slid into a sheugh [a soft verge with water course in it) his driver's door was obstructed and he had to be extricated with difficulty through the small window on the passenger side. It was such a tight squeeze that his hands and arms had to come first, then his head and shoulders. Since he was some height up, he had to be supported as he was extracted. One farmer, who helped, treated the rescue hilariously and declared: 'This is like calving a cow!'

Carters driving horses pulling heavy drays thronged Belfast docks area and the main city thoroughfares around Castle Junction in the 1920s. They were an aggressive breed. They regarded themselves as monarchs of the road, and when they mounted the forebars of their 'four-wheelers' cracked their whips and moved off, they never had the slightest regard for who or what was behind them. The wellbeing of their horses, straining to keep the heavily laden 'four-wheelers' on the move as their iron-shod hooves clattered and slipped on the granite square setts and the steel tram tracks, was the driver's sole preoccupation. Halts had to be avoided at all costs and even tram drivers gave way to these heavily-laden drays.

When motorists began to invade the pitch in the twenties, the carters did their best to squeeze them out. This cold war lasted for more than a decade. As the driver of a 'Baby Austin', in pre-war days the writer once learnt that perspex semaphore trafficators weren't designed to withstand a dunt from the iron-clad corner of one of Wordie's drays!

James Mulholland's eldest daughter, Maureen, (Mrs. Kennedy) vividly recalls being ferried to Crumlin Road courthouse by her father for her first driving licence while she was still a teenager, and having then been put behind the wheel of the ancient Model T lorry. This had the accelerator mounted as a stick on the steering column, solid tyres and almost equally solid cushions. The vehicle was without a gear box or self-starter, and when the engine stalled her father had to get out and crank it. The solid tyres were a greater menace to her on the square setts and tramlines than steel shoes were for the horses. When her wheels slipped and slithered, a skid was almost impossible to correct. Driving lessons were unheard of in those days and there were no driving tests.

The Belfast carters reactions when a teenage lassie first appeared around Queen's Quay driving a converted Model T Ford laden with a bulky load of yeast hampers would definitely not have been very cordial. Had she forced any of them to stop, their language would hardly have been printable.

Those who were around Aghagallon in the 1920s chuckle when they think of 'Judge's oul lorry which whistled. You would have known it anywhere.' Judge was the competitor of Mulholland and apparently his ancient motor vehicle made rather odd noises.

In later years, Mulholland acquired an REO Speedwagon. He still had this when the American G.I.s were around during the Second World War and he regularly received visits from interested members of the U.S. Army (G.I.s) who were stationed locally and who came from the area in the U.S.A. where the vehicles were manufactured.

Jimmy Matchett (already mentioned), and who is now in his eighties, has lively recollections of the days when he delivered potato baskets and skips for various local basket-makers. For Big Mulholland he often delivered potato baskets to McElderry & Moffatt of Ballymoney. Once he had to make two such journeys on the same day. He reckons he would have shifted 200 dozen baskets that day for a few pounds. He had a 2$^{1}/_{2}$ ton Fordson lorry with a platform which was about 14$^{1}/_{2}$ foot long and he extended this with planks to accommodate baskets.

He also went to Newcastle and Kilkeel with baskets for the Mulhollands of Gawley's Gate. Once a kind lady made tea for them at a wee place on the County Down coast. In recognition of her kindness the owner of the baskets who accompanied him gave the lady a free basket but when he was turning his lorry, Jimmy accidentally ran down the woman's dog, whereupon she turned on them fiercely and they had to make a fast get-away.

On another occasion, he came on a Derryclone basket-maker named Creaney in trouble near Rathfriland. The latter had converted an Austin saloon into a goods

49

vehicle which had stalled on Rathfriland hill, run back and 'cowped' (overturned) with a load of potato baskets on board.

Jimmy also conveyed skips to the Mersey boat at Belfast harbour for 'Big James', on occasions. He also used to deliver baskets to a greengrocer called McNabney who had a shop at Bridge End in Belfast and to another shop on the Shankill Road, next door to Hall's factory. Walsh of Derryash (Cairn Hall) supplied those two Belfast shops. On one occasion he took a load of potato baskets to the Lammas Fair at Ballycastle for 'Big James'.

He remembers seeing Creaney's carters leaving George's Island for Belfast shipyard with loads of rods at about 10 o'clock at night and he says they wouldn't have been back until ten the next night. Tom Creaney took the train from Ballinderry station in the morning and met them at Queen's Island. They had unusually big horses which they used to get shod at Knox's in Aghalee.

Jimmy never made baskets but he says he learned how to set one up. He made creels for trapping birds for the pot which was his sole experience of basket-making.

Marketing

As well as inheriting the skills of the craft, James Mulholland also inherited some useful marketing expertise from his parents and he attended the principal local markets, in season. The main potato-growing areas in his day were around Limavady, Ballymena, Ballymoney, Comber, Newry, Banbridge, Lisburn and Dromore, but he also travelled to some of the principal market towns in the South when he got a motor lorry. He sold on the streets direct to farmers and also to leading hardware stores. The season was short, say, from July or August to October for the shops, and even shorter for direct sales to growers. 'Big James' usually carried a considerable stock in a large hanger in the farmyard.

In the mid 1920s potato baskets were fetching half-a-crown (12½p) or three shillings (15p) apiece retail. Ten years later the price had doubled. Most growers made them do more than one season by carefully scraping or washing the mud off them, and hanging them up in a barn. But on most farms the potato basket was used for very many purposes for which it had never been intended.

'Big James's' eldest son, also called James, constantly accompanied his father on selling trips after he left the primary school, and he began driving the lorry once he was old enough to get a licence. He recalls taking loads of yeast hampers to Avoniel distillery in Belfast and also putting loads on the Belfast to Ardrossan boats at Belfast docks for Glenocal (he thinks) in Scotland. The REO lorry carried 40 dozen stacked in bales of six.

Later, baskets for use as cages for stone whiskey jars, and replacement lids for wooden apple barrels were also made and marketed. J.J. Hunter, McAlister and Holywood & Donnelly were customers for the baskets for whiskey jars.

At one stage, 'Big James's' brother, Willie, made skips and delivered them on behalf of his brother, but like all the other local basket-makers, Willie mostly made skips for Judge as 'Big James' had done before he engaged in direct selling to Avoniel. Willie and his family had as well a big business in potato baskets for years.

Stories which I have been given reveal the calibre of 'Big James'. Once when he had a lorry-load of potato baskets in Banbridge market he was unable to get a buyer. Another neighbour from Aghagallon was in the same boat and by afternoon James decided to store his baskets down a publican's yard. The other man wasn't so keen. He needed ready money and he was afraid of having to pay for storage. James bid him a bad price and, rather than take the load home, the other man accepted. When James got the baskets stacked on the publican's premises he went inside for a drink – got talking to a few regulars and before he finished he made a few phone calls and sold the whole consignment to a Newry customer at a fair price.

Labour

When James Mulholland set up his factory he had the ball at his toe, as far as recruitment went. There was no other insurable employment available in the locality. In fact, very little of any kind. Farm labourers, domestic servants and self-employed workers were outside the scope of the unemployment insurance scheme at that time and even the sick and disabled were living on a pittance. Some men might have had five shillings a week (25p) sick pay as voluntary contributors to Friendly Societies, but most of them would have been dependent on Poor Law relief (again only a few shillings a week).

Seventy years on, Alfred Grant often recalls how 'it was a Godsend' to him when he got into Mulholland's workshop. He had just walked out of employment with a local farmer who had cut his wages – on grounds of economy. He was determined not to work for less than he had had in spite of his mother's tears. She badly needed the money. Without it they were facing virtual starvation.

"The work was very hard," he says, "and it was very cold sitting all day in a cold shed, at Mulholland's. The pay was bad but there was no way anyone could have bettered himself. James Mulholland did us all a good turn. He did the same for the farmers by buying rods from them, for they were getting it tight too."

There was no need for 'Big James' to look for labour. Applicants beat a path to his door and through local knowledge he had the measure of every man in the catchment area, which was small due to the lack of public transport. Having grown up at Gawley's Gate he got a lot of men from that locality and a bit beyond. I have been told that the higher skilled men (the potato basket-makers) all came from around there. Men from nearer Aghagallon village centre where the factory was located, mostly made skeps only. Few of them were good at making baskets. There is just a hint here that the traditional inherited basket-making skills may have been more concentrated in the immediate lough shore area.

There were rather more Catholics than Protestants in the catchment area and this was reflected in the constitution of the labour force. Seemingly there was plenty of crack and ballads of all political flavours were sung – but no aggro.

There was no organised training, but there was relatively easy access to the workshops for aspirant basket-makers who would not have been prevented from trying their hands at rod weaving, so long as they didn't impede anybody else. They could also have practised at home. If they showed promise they would have got in, when there was room. James packed men in every corner of the workshop when he was under pressure from customers.

There does not seem to have been any mass movement of self-employed basket-makers into the factory. The Judge buyers who were in opposition kept unit rates attractive to combat poaching. They and Mulholland also competed for rods grown locally and matched each other's prices.

Miss Judge was the Principal of the Judge firm which had premises at Middlepath Street. Her brother, Joe, was her driver and he was a familiar figure around Aghagallon. During the 1939–45 war, a Belfast family named Judge took up residence at Aghagallon after the air raids. They were relatives of Miss Judge and had made friends with local people through the basket trade. One of them married an Aghagallon lady.

Some older men who had been handloom weavers in earlier life joined Mulholland's workforce. (The upright and urbane William Cinnamond is particularly well remembered.) 'Big James' also got some men who would not have been robust enough for outdoor work. T.B. was rife and it claimed a share of these men. In many instances more than one member of the same family died young. No women were recruited, but some female members of the Mulholland families helped their parents with basket-making on occasions. These included 'Big James's' sisters.

As was to be expected, the workforce eventually became restive over pay. Some say a threat of a cut in remuneration triggered off unrest eventually. The late Mick Casey, a Lurgan-based TGWU official, then organised them. There was a strike and a confrontation in the early 1930s. It was a seven-day wonder locally. The late George Moore, the then Manager of Lurgan Unemployment Exchange, personally visited the factory. That was quite something in those days! Alfred Grant, the only survivor remains reticent and obviously feels that the episode is best forgotten. Others have spoken of a man having been disallowed unemployment benefit when he refused work at a reduced pay, and of a big occasion in Lurgan when the case went to an Appeal Tribunal with Mick Casey as advocate. Some say, 'The Big Fellow was bate'. Some say he won. Anyhow, when attractive alternative employment eventually became available in the late 1930s, with the outbreak of war, it changed the whole ball game. The small factory which had been such a boon to the local job market for a quarter of a century, rapidly lost its labour force.

In terms of the present (1991) cost of creating new jobs, 'Big James' had made a very significant contribution to the local economy. The employment he created had been constant and though it was not well paid, neither was there better money elsewhere in those days. Significantly, some of his workers who switched to working for Judge returned to Mulholland again after an interval. Alex Grant had a small satellite workshop in opposition for a while but that group broke up and most of them seem to have resumed work with 'Big James'.

As has already been mentioned, no evidence of any

significant movement of basket-makers who had been self employed into the factory has been found. Of those named below only about seven had been self employed basket-makers and of these two were nephews of 'Big James'. Names of Mulholland's workforce who are remembered include:

John Barnes, Derryarnish,
Hugh Totten, Goudy Bridge (Drumaleet)
Big Joe Corey, Islands (Drumaleet)
Eddie Fegan, Turtle Dove Lock (Lagan Canal)
John, Jim and Paul Harbison, Derrynaseer
Ned McConaghy, Derrymore
Jack Mallon, Derrymore
Harry Mallon, Derrymore
Nealie Henderson, Derryclone
Ned Doran, Derryhirk
Joe, Pat and Willie Hannon (brothers), Moss Road, Derryarnish
Eddie Dougherty, Feumore
John Brennan, Colane
Alex Grant, Derryarnish
Alfred Grant, Derryarnish,
Jimmy Ferguson, Derrynaseer
John Lavery, Derryarnish,
Jimmy Johnston, Brankinstown
Joe Finnegan, Maghernagaw
Willie and Jimmy Mulholland, Derrymore
Frank McGrann (alias McKeveney) Deerpark
John Brankin and his son, Deerpark
William John Cinnamond, Islands and his son, William James
Jimmy Cinnamond, Islands (Drumaleet)
Arthur and Bill Mulholland, Gawley's Gate (nephews of 'Big James')
Jimmy Lavery, Derrynaseer and
Charlie Knox, Derrynaseer

A disabled ex-serviceman from Lurgan called David Harte, has also been mentioned. Seemingly, he was trained by some of the ex-service organisations and 'Big James' used his skill on occasions when he needed extra help.

Early nineteenth century Census records show that a large number of people in Aghagallon called Lavery were engaged in basket-making. Laverys were very numerous in Aghagallon in 'Big James's' day, and they still are, but few people of that name worked for him. Johnny of Goudy Bridge and his four sons, Joe, Sean, Arthur and Peter all worked occasionally for 'Big James', either on the farm or at baskets and so did Jimmy of Derrynaseer, but I have no record of any others.

In 'Big James's' day there were no road names or house numbers around the locality, hence nicknames had to be used to distinguish the many families of Lavery who lived locally. I have been given the following nicknames: 'The Hawk', 'The Star', 'The Kite', 'Blue cap', 'Ribs',

'Double Ribs', 'The Cute', 'The Badger', 'Plumber', 'Jingler', 'Smell the Weather', 'Tailor', 'The Postman', 'The Clout', 'Calf Tam', 'Yella Dan', and of course, 'Anthony Duck', a colourful man of the road whose story I told in *Memories of Old Lurgan*. Not one basket-maker was included in the litany of nicknames.

Although the Mulhollands were also very numerous, I have not heard of many of them having had nicknames like the Laverys.

The 1990 basketmaker's tools courtesy of David Moore, Aghagallon. The slab of lead is used to beat the weave into shape. Photo P. Smyth

The Run Down

No clear employment pattern emerged from research into the history of the basket-makers who left Mulholland's employment when the factory began to run down early in the Second World War. When wire baskets for potatoes went on sale at Aghalee general store, around that time, the writing was on the wall. They spelled the end for the traditional wicker basket which, it must be said, became over-heavy in wet harvesting conditions.

Local demand for yeast hampers had ceased over a decade before, with the closure of Avoniel distillery, and when war started space for them on cross-channel boats became almost impossible to procure, putting the Scottish market for yeast hampers in jeopardy. Many of Mulholland's workers did not wait to be laid off. Attractive rates of wages were being offered by construction firms and there was almost a mass exodus of strong men to places like Aldergrove, Langford Lodge and Maghaberry airfields, where demand for heavy labourers was high. It was in a sense a matter of the departure of the fittest. Heavy spade and shovel work was all that was available and there was a lot of hardship involved in cycling long distances morning and evening, but the wages were tempting.

Some other workers were approaching retirement age when the war started, or at least past middle age and not very fit for heavy work. They would have signed-on at the Employment Exchange or claimed sickness benefit or retirement pensions. Means-tested Unemployment Assistance was by that time available to supplement national insurance benefits or provide maintenance for people who had drawn out unemployment benefit.

To summarise, Alfred Grant became an auxiliary postman, another man went to a local animal products factory, another went to Dunmurry bacon factory, a fourth got a job as a joiner with the local authority. A few went to work for farmers (minimum wages had by that time been prescribed by law). One took up self-employment as a travelling grocer. Another went on the road as a general dealer, using a pony and van. One started to hawk paraffin oil from a horse-drawn van. A few resumed self-employment in the fancy basket sector. A number had already succumbed to the ravages of T.B. before the War.

The outbreak of war had changed the outlook for 'Big James'. His labour force had begun to disperse in pursuit of higher wages and when a War Department contract became available he decided not to tender. It went to a man from across the water, one source says his name was Mayer, who put a local man, Frank McGrann, in charge of a small factory which was housed in a Nissen hut at Deerpark. There panniers for dropping supplies from aeroplanes were manufactured in sizeable quantities. James

Mulholland of Moss Road who is still in the trade worked in Frank McGrann's factory.

Although he was in his sixties by then and beginning to slow down a bit, 'Big James' remained active. By that time he had acquired more land and bought the local village store. His daughters looked after the place but purchasing and overall management probably remained with 'the boss'. Concurrently he extended his mixed farming activities with the advent of compulsory tillage Orders.

His workforce had scattered and demand for potato baskets was sharply reduced. As well he had eventually to give up striving to get space for skeps on the cross-channel boats. Fortunately, the advent of war had stopped imports of wickerware and James wasn't slow to exploit the new opportunities which arose for import substitution.

He and his family were soon deeply involved in the manufacture of all kinds of other wickerware, including chairs. James bought a second-hand rod_ peeling machine from some concern at Crumlin Road, Belfast, which was closing down. He also got an oversized rectangular boiler made to boil osiers, and various tinplate trays, with handles over them, for dyeing rods. He boiled peeled rods to give them a buff appearance and experimented with 'Drummer' textile dyes. These were no use, but he managed to get suitable wood dyes and eventually turned out a wide variety of colours. Osiers were first split, then planed, wrapped in coils, and boiled in dye.

As was the case when he was making potato baskets, 'Big James' soon achieved a degree of excellence in making small baskets which none of his family was able to match. Until his health failed with advancing years, he remained the craftsman par excellence.

Remains of ancient rod peeling machine built rather like a barn threshing machine and power driven, to be seen at Mulholland's premises. It was bought second-hand from a party who were in business at Crumlin Road, Belfast, circa 1945. Someone from New Zealand bought the teeth (tines) some years ago. Photo: P Smyth, 1990.

The Competitors

In the present century there were at least four small basket factories in Aghagallon parish, all owned by parties called Mulholland. 'Big James' as we know was at the junction of the three townlands of Aghagallon, Derrynaseer and Ballykeel on the B12, at the end of what is now Goudy Bridge Road.

James's father, William, and later his brother, William, was making baskets at the old homestead at Gawley's Gate and James's brother, Tom was a short distance away also in Derryola making baskets. As well Willie and James Mulholland, another Mulholland family (no relation), were busy in a council cottage on the Derrymore Road facing Bartin's Bay. They remained in the craft all their lives and as recently as the nineteen-sixties one of them took part in a trade show in New York organised by the then Stormont Department of Commerce.

Some five miles from Aghagallon towards Crumlin and contemporaneously with 'Big James's' enterprise, another man named Mulholland was engaged in basket-making at Upper Ballinderry. This man, Isaac, also started from humble beginnings and went from success to success. Tradition has it that he had received so little schooling that he was virtually illiterate and he was 60 years of age and a rich man before he signed his first cheque.

Apparently he was hired to a North Antrim farmer in his youth. Then he and Davy Burns of Glenavy went to Antrim hiring fair another time. Davy got hired but Isaac didn't so he came home and started to the baskets. He started not so far from Upper Ballinderry crossroads in what is now the A26.

Later he bought a prestigious place at Devlin's Hill, called 'Chestnutt House' (a public house and farm). This property is still in the family and it is at the rear of the pub that the remains of the of the old basket factory still stand. It is a two storeyed building and it once housed a dozen or more basket-makers. There are still some vintage base boards and lengths of rib timber lying around.

Names of men who worked there include: John and Billy Walsh (brothers); Robbie Cinnamond and his son; a wee man named Gallery; Samuel James Crossey and Joe Hannon. That would have been in the 1920s.

Isaac started off with horse-drawn vehicles – a haycart with long trams and a cage over the horses rump is remembered. He sent goods from nearby Ballinderry railway station and Judge's lorry also called. Skeps and potato baskets were made – yeast skeps, bread skeps and wicker baskets as covers for glass spirit jars. Some went to Judge, some to G.B. and some to McGleenon's Bakery in Belfast.

Isaac bought rods from Creaney of George's Island.

An ancient ledger which is in the possession of Dan Mulholland, a grandson of Isaac's, contains a lot of entries relating to 'rolls of hamper', 'bundles of baskets', and 'bundles of rods'. For example:

Dec. 1. 1931:	67 bundles of baskets – 16/6. 3 doz.
	baskets 1/6, 3 bundles rods 1/-
12/12/31:	67 rolls hampers 16/6
7/9/31:	15 doz. baskets at 5/-

Unfortunately the records do not show the destination. McGleenon's Bakery is thought to have bought hampers. The money entries in the ledger probably represent freight charges; 16/6 means sixteen shillings and 6 pence ($82^1/2$p).

Robbie (Bob) Cinnamond was Chairman of a local Gaelic Football Club, 'The Owen Roes', and they held club meetings in Isaac's workshop. They also travelled to away-matches in Isaac's Thornycroft lorry, which had solid tyres. These facts were included in the *History of the G.A.A. in Glenavy (1910–198??)*, which was published some years back. The book features a picture of the 'Thornycroft' lorry laden with potato baskets.

A family named Crossey, who lived in a council cottage near Chestnutt House made a particularly good range of fancy baskets when Isaac was in the trade.

John McAlinden, who is inclined to be economical with words, put it thus when he was asked to say just how many of his immediate neighbours around Bartin's Bay had got involved:

"As many as cud get at them. It was a right wintertime job but it wasn't a warm one, working with oul wet rods, unless you had a bay of a house that you were able to light a fire in. Mulholland had to put fireplaces in his workshops eventually. The men cudn't stick the cold."

John McAreavey of Aghadalgon unearthed these artefacts. The sledgehammer and wedges are easily identifiable, also the tongs for stripping the bark off rods. The odd-looking tool with the makeshift handle is a splitter. All were used to cleave fir timber to make ribs for baskets.

Photo: P. Smyth.

"There was nothing to it. I did it for a wee while, but not for long. You just got a bit of a board and put holes in to hold the posts. Then you weaved the oul rods. Some of them weaved them in handfuls. The skeps were every shape, not like a tradesman's job at all. They never came back. They only made the one trip.

"Spud-baskets were a different thing altogether. Not so many were good at them. Anybody cud have made a skep."

John is a fisherman at heart and one who was an expert at a very young age at looping eel hooks on lines and laying the lines out in an orderly fashion so that they would not snag when they were being played out. He doesn't think the men who made skeps needed skill at all.

I am indebted to Gerard McAreavey of Johnston Park, Glenavy, and formerly of Aghadalgon, for useful and comprehensive notes on the basket-making trade which flourished in the Sandy Bay and Aghadalgon area nearer Glenavy in the latter end of the 19th century and continued until 1960. Gerard's father, Samuel, (born 1887) of Store Quay, Sandy Bay, started making baskets when he was 12 years of age at his brother-in-law, Sammy Courtney's place at nearby Aghadalgon, where the original workshop is still standing. Samuel came of fishermen stock and he set up a workshop at Store Quay when he was about 16 years of age.

In 1918, he acquired a 17-acre farm at Aghadalgon, which is still in family ownership. Eventually he married and had eleven of a family, seven boys and four girls, born between 1923 and 1945. Samuel pursued the trade of growing osiers, making basketware and marketing it on a fair scale at Aghadalgon up until 1960 and all the family were involved. The older boys, all became skilled craftsmen. The younger ones and the girls bottomed baskets set up by Harry Brazier and helped with the cutting of osiers and other related tasks. Harry Brazier, a brother-in-law of Samuel's helped. Joe Hannon, Bob Nelson and Paddy Brankin all of Ballyvannon were employed as well – also Bob Cinnamond of Aghadalgon.

Joe Brankin of Feumore, Tom McCartney of Spinnymore and Harry Meekin of Ballymacraven (all of these are nearby townlands).

Lizzie Courtney, happily still alive at the age of 90, a niece of Sam's also bottomed baskets at McAreavey's workshop.

Sam McAreavey specialised in potato baskets, for which he found an outlet at Elliott's of Portaferry, but apple hampers and hurdles were made as well. He acquired a motor lorry for deliveries and Harry Brazier drove this until William's son, John, was old enough to take over. He sold skeps to Judge.

Sam's rod house (workshop) had an earthen floor and a coal fire. Sam's main pursuit was dealing in fowl and apples. Basket-making was a subsidiary.

Jimmy Crossey, Pat Mulholland and Pat O'Neill, all of Ballymaclose; Dan Brankin, John Brankin and John

'Horse' used for splitting fir timber to make ribs for potato baskets. Picture courtesy of Gerard McAreavey, Glenavy.

Crossey of Ballyvorley; Crawford Brankin of Ballyvannon; Dan Brankin of Derachrin; and Sam Courtney of Aghadalgon have been named as craftsmen who made baskets at home in the first half of the 20th century. Sam Courtney, a brother-in-law of Sam McAreavey, employed six or eight basket-makers and sold skeps to Judge.

An elderly man, named Solomon Courtney, son of Sam, formerly of Aghadalgon, may still be making baskets at Unity Flats, Belfast.

A road between Glenavy village and Crumlin is known as The Sally Hedge Road. Many acres of osiers were grown at Aghadalgon, Ballymacricket, Ballyvorley, Ballyvannon, Ballymaclose, Ballymacraven, Feumore, Edenturcher and other adjacent townlands, when the basket-making industry was flourishing. The rods were planted in the Spring, around 17th March and harvested in November. They were steeped in a nearby river or at

Basketmaker's draw knife owned by Gerard McAreavey, Glenavy. Photo: P. Smyth.

McAreavey's (lough) shore. In one of McAreavey's fields Sam cultivated a special class of fine rod, known as Packing Cord. Remnants of the crop still survive. They are thin, wirey and light yellow. They were used for opening or closing potato baskets and for making handles.

Neighbours used McAreavey's workshop as a kind of ceili house. There would have been great crack nearly every night and it would have continued until ten o'clock, maybe twelve, of a winter's night while work continued.

Sam McAreavey, Harry Brazier and other members of the family cut fir trees for ribs of potato baskets anywhere they could get them. Anthony Hamill of Ballymote was one supplier. Crosscut-saws operated by two men were used to cut the trees into logs and logs were split with cleavers and wooden wedges which were made at a sawmill.

A metal fender or smaller cleaver was also used for splitting rods. Three fir ribs went into the centre of the base of each potato basket.

Sam McAreavey bought rims for baskets in lots of 100 but sometimes alders or buckie briars were used. Sam measured a rim from the point of his elbow to the joint of his little finger and then tied it across.

Draw knives and shoemakers' knives were used to pare ribs and a pair of metal tongs (called 'strippers') were used for peeling rods.

Two wooden contraptions known as a horse and a mare were used as trestles when rib timber was being split (cleaved) and shaved. "The horse stood up but you sat on the mare." These are illustrated on page 61 and it will be seen that the horse was a fairly simple contraption resembling the traditional farm trestle which farmers used to support shafts of loaded carts and other things around the haggard. The mare was a much more complicated animal. One still survives (1991) at McAreavey's of Aghadalgon and is in a good state of preservation (see page 66). Another is to be found in a farm museum near Frensdorf, Bamberg in Bavaria.

In the 1950s fancy baskets were made in a workshop at Edenturcher which was originally a flax mill. Sam McAreavey Junior, Mick Crossey and Harry Brazier, Mick Brankin and Barney McKavanagh (of Aghagallon) wrought at them.

Vincent Crossey of Ballymaclose, whose father made fancy baskets still grows osiers at Station Road, Ballymaclose. Johnny Crossey of Edenturcher, who worked for Isaac Mulholland up to 1930, was known locally as 'basket Johnny'. Isaac was in the basket trade for about 25 years from 1905 until 1930.

The Wheel turns Full Circle

In the period of just under 80 years which has elapsed since 'Big James' Mulholland took the plunge and moved from the hearth to a factory the wheel has turned full circle. Skeps are now museum pieces and any potato baskets which are made nowadays are for household use. But the second strand of the craft, i.e. fancy basketware still lives on. One man deserves credit for that and by coincidence his name is also James Mulholland. James still cultivates osiers for his own use.

What is even more interesting is the fact that he works alone at Moss Road close to Gawley's Gate and Grant's Lane on the hearth of what was until recently the family home. Moss Road is a quiet loanen in the heart of the Montiaghs and to step into the low whitewashed house by the roadside where the highest grade of fancy baskets are on display is like putting the clock back for generations. That is not to suggest that James has not moved with the times. On the contrary, he is equally adept at weaving modern or reproduction wickerware.

The working life of this James Mulholland spans the period of half a century which has elapsed since the run down of 'Big James's' factory and details are therefore, of particular interest. When he left school he tried his hand at making skeps in 'Big James's' factory. Since his uncle, Paddy Hannon, was a long established worker there he would have had no difficulty in getting a job.

*James Mulholland of Moss Road, Aghagallon, who cultivates osiers and makes baskets of every description on the hearth in the traditional style. He is now the only full-time basket maker in the area and has acted as tutor at further education classes locally. He has been making baskets for almost half a century. Here he is making up a bale of Church Collection baskets.
Photo: P. Smyth, 1991.*

He stayed only three weeks. (Skeps would have been on the way out.) Then he joined Alex Grant's team at a small workshop nearer home, at Grants' Lane. Johnny Barnes, and Big Ned McConaghy were there already making potato baskets for Judge. He learned the art of making a potato basket there but again he did not stay long, and for a year or so after that he made fancy baskets at home.

A selection of baskets displayed by James Mulholland of Moss Road (1991). Mostly made from osiers grown by himself locally, they include Church Collection baskets, child's cradle ('Moses Basket'), shopping baskets and log baskets. Baskets for phaetons, armour for Armagh Mummers (Rimers), a basket for a vintage invalid carriage are other examples of his versatility. Photo: P. Smyth.

When Frank McGrann (McKavanagh) got the job of foreman in a war time workshop which was set up in a disused potato house at Mairs' farm at the Deerpark he asked James to join him and he agreed. Panniers suitable for dropping supplies from aircraft were made in that factory. There were fairly well designed articles, made from stripped osiers (white and buff), painted and strapped. Later, he wove wicker armchairs which had a circular seat and a diamond pattern. A business man (Mr. Mayer) who owned a pram factory in Belfast is said to have been the Principal of the Deerpark enterprise.

At the end of the war when the Deerpark venture went out of business, James resumed self employment making fancy baskets. He was able to keep going until about 1969 when demand dropped off.

In 1977 an order for baskets from Mr. and Mrs. Kirk who owned an antique and craft shop at Ballinderry enabled him to get going again. An order from a Crawfordsburn craft shop followed. Mr. Kirk incidentally, hails from Derryclone originally and his father cultivated a large acreage of rods when demand was high.

James is now widely recognised as a master craftsman. A basket for a vintage phaeton to be seen at the Ulster Folk Museum is an example of his work. Armour worn by the Armagh Mummers (Rimers) is another. Some more of his work can be seen at Ardress House, County Armagh. Interestingly some of his wares may soon form the foundation of an Irish exhibit at the German basket museum

David Moore, grandson of 'Big James', demonstrates a hand-held gadget for stripping bark off rods, one at a time. David uses a modern cabinet-type machine for bulk stripping. Photo: P. Smyth, 1990.

at Michelau (see appendices).

Now nearing retirement age, James is conscious of the need to hand on his skill to a succeeding generation. To this end he has participated in a scheme of further education which was set up locally by acting as tutor in basket-making. The level of interest has not been very encouraging,

but if a training scheme to provide allowances were to be organised the response might be better. James's near neighbour and cousin, Christie Hannon, a son of the late Paddy Hannon, was one of those who attended the further education course and he has tried his hand at the craft and at cultivating osiers.

David Moore, also of Moss Road now (he has moved), makes fine basketware as a sideline. He and James Mulholland are the only stalwarts who are now keeping the fancy basket craft alive locally, which is a pity as demand is encouraging.

A selection of baskets made in 1990 by David Moore, grandson of 'Big James' Mulholland. David is a fine craftsman who makes baskets as a subsidiary occupation. He is now residing at Moss Road, Gawley's Gate. Photo: P. Smyth.

The Bavarian Scene

When I thought I had finished my research I decided to go on vacation. Fortuitously I found myself in a region steeped in the craft, with baskets everywhere. When on a visit to Bamberg in Bavaria I discovered that I was in the heart of the German basket-making region. In Bamberg the traditional Lenten basket fair is a big event where all the local craftsmen exhibit their wares.

A 'mare' and a draw knife on display at Frensdorf Museum in Bavaria. Photo: P. Smyth, 1991.

There is a farm museum (Bauernmuseum) at Frensdorf, ten miles south of Bamberg where wickerware artefacts are featured widely. I was excited to find a wooden contraption at Frensdorf almost identical to one which Gerard McAreavey's of Glenavy showed me. County Antrim basket-makers called it 'a mare' and it is featured in this book. There was a draw knife on display in the Bauernmuseum as well, similar to a Glenavy specimen.

The German basket museum at Michelau about twenty miles north of Bamberg fascinated me. Exhibits on display illustrate the history of basket-making over a period of more than 5000 years, some based on imprints found in clay, dating from the ice age. The range of basketware on display at Michelau is enormous and I need not attempt to catalogue it here. Not only does it feature all Germany, in all ages, but Africa, Asia, America, India etc., are featured as well.

I was particularly interested in the exhibits of tools and equipment and a mock-up of a traditional cottage workshop which was on display, together with raw material which includes fir, oak and hazel, in addition to willow. I found some baskets closely resembling the Ulster potato basket but none had the two side handles with which we are familiar. One oval basket had holes at either end corresponding to a description given to me by Alfred

Grant. It had timber ribs resembling strips of fir of the Ulster type.

At Küps near Lichtenfels on the way to Coburg, I found a factory warehouse with a most comprehensive display. It had basketware of every age, size and shape. Some tiny dolls' prams were obviously very old. Sets of closely-woven furniture of the Chesterfield suite style seemed modern and there was much between. Again, I found baskets there like our own potato baskets but without the side handles. Possibly the muscular Bavarians scorned the notion of two people lifting one basket and used one with a single, arched handle.

My son-in-law, Werner Heikenwälder, who was my guide and interpreter on the tour, has told me that he remembers willow being cultivated by his grandfather at Merkendorf near Bamberg. His grandfather made baskets for his everyday needs from them.

My experience of Bavaria has left me wondering why the basket-making industry has almost died out on Lough Neagh's banks. In 1907, four per cent of the whole population of Germany was employed in the industry mostly in the Saxon Coburg region. I do not have more up-to-date figures but since two factories at Michelau now have a combined labour force of 800 hand crafting basketware it is obviously still very much alive.

The beauty and practical appeal of its modern products put plastics in the shade. If the Bavarians can compete with wire, plastic, and low-cost imports, maybe there is hope

Kirsten Heikenwälder, the author's Bavarian granddaughter, and her mum, Aileen, display an artefact at the farm museum at Frensdorf near Bamberg, May 1991. Photo: P. Smyth.

still for our own native craft. The skill has survived into the present generation but in another it could perish. Ditto, the graceful willow rod which still grows on the banks of the derelict Lagan canal – eight or nine feet high and not a branch on it. That's what the traditional craftsman yearns to handle ... pliable as silk and almost as beautiful when woven by a Master basket-maker. Even the smell of a new osier basket has a magic of its own.

Bavarian ladies favour wicker shopping baskets instead of the polythene bags which litter our environment and they even use containers resembling the traditional Ulster potato basket filled with flowers to hang from the porches of their beautiful houses. With a bit of aggressive marketing maybe our own basket-makers could regain a slot in the market and save the craft from dying out.

These baskets are exhibited at the German Basket Museum. The type on the right is often filled with flowers and suspended from the porches of houses in Bavaria. Photo: P. Smyth, 1991.

Epilogue – Down Memory's Lane

It is only since I have begun handling potato baskets again recently that I have come to realise just how much of my boyhood memories are enshrined in them. From my earliest days, until I left the farm as a young man in 1945, potato baskets were in daily use. Just before I left, I acquired an old banger of a motor bike, and dismantled the engine. It was into an old potato basket, lined with sacking, that I put all the pieces in case I lost some on the workshop floor. In the event, I had a few over when I thought I had it correctly re-assembled! But I was 'mis-using' potato baskets long before that.

My mother used an over-size potato basket as a clothes' basket. (She had no nylons or dainty lingerie to snag.) I recall being chivvied as a toddler for climbing into a basket, and using it as a rocker with my legs dangling over the end of it.

My father was adept at balancing a full basket on his hip, and also at pouring the contents into the narrow mouth of a potato sack, without spillage. Many a time I had to carry the hurricane lamp for him on a winter's evening as he carried turnips to the pulper and pushed an empty potato basket below the machine with his toe to collect the pulp for the cows.

The potato baskets were indispensable when the apples were ripe. A cushion of clean corn straw (not hay, which breeds mites) had to be used for the soft Kemp apples. The hardy Brambley seedlings just got the bare basket. But anyone who is familiar with the rich aroma of the Kemp will realise why they got kid glove treatment. Once we laid them singly on the floor of the attic, their sweet presence was unmistakable.

Even the worn-out basket which had shed its bottom, was not without use. At home one was regularly used to protect some 'clockin' hen as she sat on her eggs in the corner of the outhouse. Mind you, my father didn't let the bottom rot out of many baskets. He had special wooden pegs which he used as scalpels to clean all the soil off them, and the new or nearly-new ones, were carefully scraped and washed clean before they were stored away. Only the older ones were allowed to be used for odd jobs.

Two scenes in particular have been vividly recalled by the sight of Alfred's basket. Its newness has reminded me of the thrill of my father's unloading a bale of newly-bought ones from the horse-drawn van. They came in a bale, like a stack of hats for a hatter's shelf, mid-green in colour with the distinctive odour of freshly-cut osiers. Each a thing of beauty contrasting with the earthy environment of the farmyard. When the bale was opened, I remember as a small boy being allowed to use an upturned one as a stool. We weren't allowed to sit on an old one – for obvious reasons. The bottom would have caved in; with age they became very brittle. That was the advantage of new baskets. They were virtually indestructible. Mind you, we didn't get some every year.

The second scene is set at the far end of the sand field on my father's farm, near Morrow's Hill. Two bay horses attached to a potato-digger stand docilely in mid-field. Another horse, a 20-year-old black one, called Paddy, is grazing at the ditch back, wearing cart harness. Three carts are spaced out: one at the middle and one at either end of the potato plot. A drill has just been scattered, and the bright blue Aran Victory crop glistens in the thin rays of October sunshine. It is evening and there is a trace of frost, which sharpens every sound – so much so that the steam train, puffing and protesting as it ascends Beckett's Hill, and chortling with glee as it runs downhill beyond it, towards Lurgan, sounds as if it were in the next field, whereas it is nearly a mile away. The pungent small of freshly—spread soil and potato stalks is very invigorating. There are six members of the family working in pairs, each pair with a basket, gathering the harvest – my older brothers and my father. I am too young to be useful, but allowed to help my Dad. Soon he interrupts picking the potatoes to fetch Paddy to draw home a loaded cart. When he sets off, I plod along behind, swinging on the tram of the cart. A loud grind from the wheels tells me that we are out on the road. My father has the reins tied to the forebar, for Paddy needs no driver. The aroma of Clarke's perfect plug tobacco floats back to me, from my father's pipe. Perhaps it was the gathering frost which caused me to notice it that time, in particular, for I was well used to it. On the way back, I get a ride in the empty cart and I am even allowed to drive. Paddy doesn't need to be told that there is a rookie on the flight-deck. He just plods on, regardless of which rein I pull. He knows what he has to do – an achievement which was to come in very useful, very soon.

I had no means of foreseeing then that within one week I was destined to make a vastly different trip, behind another jet black horse, but with a very different equipage. On this occasion there was to be no grind of iron-shod wheel on stone; no clink of trace-chain on shaft. All would be silent, except for the sound of the horse's hooves as the rubber-tyred carriage purred along; instead of the wind in my hair there was to be the stuffy polish-laden atmosphere of a closed cab.

At journey's end I was to savour once more the odour of freshly-turned soil, but instead of the cheerful rumble of potatoes falling into a cart, there was to be the macabre rattle of soil and pebbles on a bare coffin lid. My father had gathered his last harvest. But at least his faithful steed, Paddy, had had the satisfaction of bringing him home safely in the trap, when the hand which held the reins had lost its grip. That was the sure grip that I had depended on for so long. Always it had been mine which had faltered, not his, as he chanted 'One, two, three – up!' while we swung a basket full of potatoes onto the cart, heeled up on its trams in the potato patch.

Acknowledgements

The extent to which I am indebted to the senior citizens who acted as narrators, to members of the Mulholland family and to the other surviving members of what, for ease of reference, I will term the local basket making community, is self evident from the text of this book. It only remains for me to record my deep appreciation.

Next I wish to thank Dr. Gailey, Dr. Crawford and Ms. Megan McManus of the Ulster Folk and Transport Museum, especially the latter two who have been the most diplomatic and skilful back seat drivers imaginable. They are largely responsible for ensuring that I kept right on to the end of the road and I am now very glad that I did. Notes compiled by Megan about early nineteenth century records have been incorporated in the text with her permission, and I am most grateful.

I could not possibly list all the other people who have helped me by answering questions and providing constructive criticism. Most of them have long been my friends and I just wish to let them know that I am not unmindful of what they have contributed.

Next I wish to thank Andy Anderson of the Ulster Folk Museum who skilfully drew the map for me. It is an essential annex and I am most grateful.

Last but not least I wish to name Mrs. Mary McKavanagh, my near neighbour, who acted as 'word processor' with great skill and patience. The final text which was prepared by Mary is a monument to her accuracy and general proficiency. Without her this work would probably never have been completed. Thank you, Mary.

Patrick Smyth